The Beginner's

Calligraphy

MARGARET MORGAN

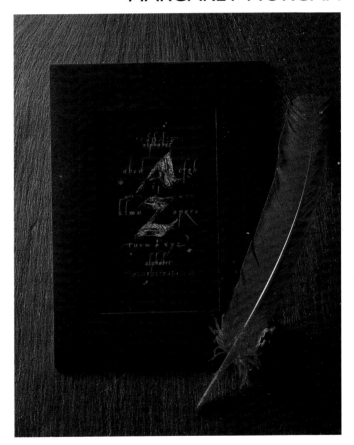

Photography by John Freeman

NEW HOLLAND

This edition first published in 2005 by
New Holland Publishers (UK) Ltd
London · Cape Town · Sydney · Auckland

Garfield House
86–88 Edgware Road
London W2 2EA
www.newhollandpublishers.com

80 McKenzie Street
Cape Town 8001
South Africa

Level 1, Unit 4
14 Aquatic Drive
Frenchs Forest, NSW 2086
Australia

218 Lake Road
Northcote
Auckland
New Zealand

1 3 5 7 9 10 8 6 4 2

Text and calligraphy designs copyright © 2001 Margaret Morgan
Photography copyright © 2001 New Holland Publishers (UK) Ltd
Copyright © 2001 New Holland Publishers (UK) Ltd

ISBN 1 85974 964 X

Editor: Clare Johnson
Design and Art Direction: Blackjacks
Photographer: John Freeman
Editorial Direction: Rosemary Wilkinson

Reproduction by Modern Age Repro House Ltd, Hong Kong
Printed and bound in Singapore by Tien Wah Press (Pte) Ltd

Every effort has been made to present clear and accurate instructions. The author and
publishers can offer no guarantee or accept any liability for any injury, illness or damage which may
inadvertently be caused to the user while following these instructions.

ACKNOWLEDGEMENTS
Grateful thanks to the following for providing the materials for photography:
Daler Rowney Ltd, Winsor & Newton, L Cornelissen & Son Ltd, Falkiner Fine Papers, Cowling & Wilcox.
Thanks also to friends and calligraphic colleagues who have guided and encouraged
me over the years, especially my patient and understanding husband.

contents

introd

Lettering is fun! This book is intended for beginners or those with just a little experience of wielding a pen. It aims to give you the information you need to write several different scripts well, and goes on to introduce the use of design in simple calligraphic projects. Once you have grasped the basic skills of good letterforms, there are so many exciting techniques and materials, both ancient and modern, to try out for yourself.

In this age when computers seem to be taking over so many things, it does no harm at all to re-examine the source of the letters we see and use every day. Look at how those 26 letters are made following traditional models, then take courage and go forward with experiments of your own. Try to be open to ideas from other cultures too; other less familiar influences than your own can inform your thinking and open up new horizons.

My involvement with calligraphy started early; learning how to do italic handwriting aged eight and a gift of some broad-edged nibs had me hooked. I studied graphic design at college, specializing in typography – letters again – and this formed the major part of my work for over ten years. The art training was certainly useful for extending the creative possibilities for the many gifts I have made over the years using letters. Those edged pens were never far away and calligraphy has now taken over completely from graphics, which gives me much satisfaction.

Calligraphy – A Guide to Hand-lettering gives you a glimpse of what is possible with pen, paper, inks and paints, with a little time, patience and enthusiasm. You may find, as I have, that your interest goes beyond the hobby stage, and is with you forever.

Margaret Morgan

uction

Monday Lundi Montag Lunedi Lunes	Tuesday Mardi Dienstag Martedi Martes	Wednesday Mercredi Mittwoch Mercoledi Micrcolès	Thursday Jeudi Donnerstag Giovedi Jueves	Friday Vendredi Freitag venerdi Viernes	Saturday Samedi Samstag Sabato Sàbado	Sunday Dimanche Sonntag Domenica Domingo
	1	2	3	4	5	6
7	8	9	10	11	12	13
14	15	16	17	18	19	20
21	22	23	24	25	26	27
28	29	30	31			

JANUARY
JANVIER
JANUARI
ENERO
GENNAIO

a brief history of
western calligraphy

The history of calligraphy, like many other histories, is cyclical: a new writing style is born, developed and eventually dies or goes out of fashion; this is followed by rediscovery, reappraisal and further improvement. What follows is only an outline of how our current letterforms came into being.

roman capitals

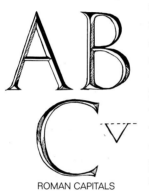

ROMAN CAPITALS

Our familiar Western letterforms mostly stem from the Roman capitals (or majuscules) of the early centuries AD. These capitals were used for important and formal inscriptions. It is generally believed that the letters were first painted with a square-edged brush, then cut into a V-section in stone. The pattern of thick and thin strokes shows the calligraphic influence of the tools used to make them and the angle at which the tools were held. They weren't "everyday" letterforms though, as they required care and precision in the making.

Square and rustic capitals fall into the same category. These early book hands were used for writing out classical texts. They were slow to write and required much pen manipulation to achieve the shapes – not natural pen-written forms at all.

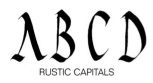

RUSTIC CAPITALS

Scribes gradually modified the capitals to economize on effort for the sake of speed; they took notes with their metal styli onto wax tablets and gradually a cursive or running hand evolved. These tablets could be smoothed over and reused after the text had been transferred to a more permanent form, such as with reeds or quills on papyrus.

SQUARE CAPITALS

uncials and half uncials

Between the 4th and 8th centuries AD, uncials developed out of the old Roman cursive hand, for writing out Christian

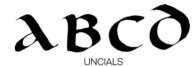

UNCIALS

texts. The forms were rounded, written with a slanted pen at a shallow angle and showed the first real suggestion of ascenders and descenders. These are the first true pen-made letters, the shapes being created by the nature of the tool, not by trying to imitate anything else. They are clear, simple and legible, and continue to provide inspiration to modern calligraphers. Later forms were written with a flat pen angle.

The spread of Christianity had much to do with the next

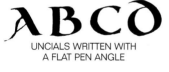

UNCIALS WRITTEN WITH
A FLAT PEN ANGLE

development of written forms. The Roman Empire began to decline into chaos, incessant wars caused further difficulties and much "pagan" classical literature was lost during the period we call the Dark Ages (AD 550–750). Cultural life in Europe more or less ceased as the barbarians invaded and care of books and teaching passed to the care of the church. Half uncials developed independently during this time in Ireland and England from early examples of Roman uncials, and show clear ascenders and descenders. The most famous examples of the different types of

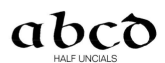

HALF UNCIALS

"insular" half uncials can be seen in the Irish *Book of Kells* and the English *Lindisfarne Gospels*.

carolingian minuscules

The Age of Charlemagne was another important milestone. The Emperor Charlemagne was passionate about books and learning. His ambition was the revival

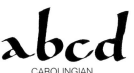

CAROLINGIAN MINUSCULES

of cultural life, for which books were essential. In AD 789 he decreed that all liturgical books should be revised. The Carolingian hand is characterized by a clear fluency and legibility which was ideal for these book texts. It was combined with the majuscules (built-up Roman letters, rustic capitals and unicals) of antiquity which were used for chapter headings, sub-headings and the beginnings of

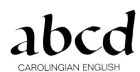

CAROLINGIAN ENGLISH

verses, the hierarchy of scripts scribes still use today.

An English version of this hand was developed as an almost perfect model for formal writing – strong forms, logically made with a consistent pen angle and easily read.

gothic

By the 12th century letterforms were becoming more and more compressed and the soft flow of Carolingian gradually gave

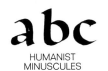

GOTHIC HAND

way to the heavy, angular black letters of northern Europe known as Gothic. Materials became more expensive as demand for books increased, so the need to economize was greatly helped by the narrow Gothic letters that took up a lot less space, but which were harder to read.

There were regional variations of the style across the European continent; the northern European quadrata had diamond feet and was very angular; rotunda, used in Spain and Italy, was much rounder in form; and the precissus Gothic of English manuscripts was characterized by its flat feet.

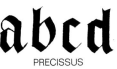

PRECISSUS

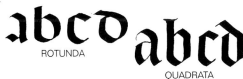

ROTUNDA

QUADRATA

the renaissance

During the Renaissance period in Italy (c.1300–1500), there was a resurgence of interest in classical literature and Italian scribes rediscovered

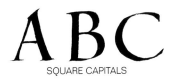

SQUARE CAPITALS

the Carolingian minuscule. They also studied the Roman inscriptional letters and Bartolommeo San Vito revived the use of square capitals, developing his own distinctive

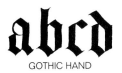

HUMANIST MINUSCULES

style. Humanist minuscules, closely based on Carolingian, with their rounded forms were very legible, dignified and perfectly suited to formal texts.

What we now call italics also emerged at this time. Written with a slight slant and fewer pen lifts, italics were oval in form and flowed elegantly and relatively swiftly from the pen, making them ideal for secretaries writing documents at speed. Italics eventually evolved into copperplate script, where thicks

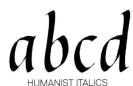

HUMANIST ITALICS

and thins are made by applying degrees of pressure to a pointed nib, a move away from true pen-written forms.

modern calligraphy

Printing with movable type was invented around the mid-15th century, but printing didn't entirely destroy the art of penmanship. Letters patent and diplomas were still produced in the traditional way. However, much of the craft fell out of use for almost two centuries, until William Morris rekindled interest in pen-lettering for the Arts and Crafts movement in the 19th-century. Morris championed the cause of the craftsman-made object in an age of increasing mass production, putting his studies of old manuscripts to good use when he set up his Kelmscott Press in 1890, in order to print beautiful and individual books. The real breakthrough for calligraphy came with the researches of Edward Johnston during the early part of the 20th century. His painstaking work brought about the rediscovery of broad-edged nibs and their importance in the development of the Western alphabet. His influence spread throughout Britain and into Europe in the 1940s and 50s, as well as to the United States.

an equipment overview

The very basic requirements for creating letterforms are pen, pencil, ink, paper and a drawing board, but before long you will probably want to add other items to your toolbox, such as some of those listed in the following pages, in order to complete the projects in this book. Buy these extra items gradually, getting the best you can afford, which will pay dividends over time. Good equipment not only gives satisfaction in use, but, as long as it is properly looked after, will last for many years.

essential equipment

To start practising calligraphy you will need just a small toolbox of essential equipment.

BRUSHES: Load nibs and mix paints with inexpensive brushes and keep the best quality sables for fine finished work (see page 15).

DIP PENS: A dip pen consists of a pen holder that can be fixed with nibs of various sizes and ink reservoirs, if required (see pages 13 and 19). It can be used with ink or paint (see page 13).

DRAWING BOARD: You will need a board at least A2 size (420 x 594 mm/16 x 23 in), preferably larger, to work on. Instead of buying a board, you can easily make your own, quite cheaply, from an offcut of MDF (see page 12).

INK: Use non-waterproof ink bought in bottles (see page 14).

MASKING TAPE: A low-tack masking tape should be used to attach paper to the drawing board surface; it can be removed easily.

METAL RULER OR STRAIGHT EDGE: This should be used for cutting paper or card with a scalpel or craft knife; a plastic ruler will be quickly damaged by sharp scalpel blades.

PAPER: You will need a variety of papers, depending on the nature of the project, as well as layout and tracing paper to make roughs (see page 18).

PENCILS: Have an H or HB handy for ruling lines (see page 15).

PLASTIC ERASER: This should be soft enough not to smudge or spoil lettering.

TRANSPARENT RULER: A 45 cm (18 in) clear plastic ruler will be the most useful for ruling lines because you can see your work through it.

useful additions

These additions to the basic toolbox will be necessary as you progress from the early writing exercises to working on the projects.

BONE FOLDER: This specialist tool is used for scoring and folding paper and is available from suppliers of bookbinding materials.

COMPASSES AND DIVIDERS: You will need these to draw circles and mark points for ruling lines. Springbow dividers have a central screw to retain a set measurement.

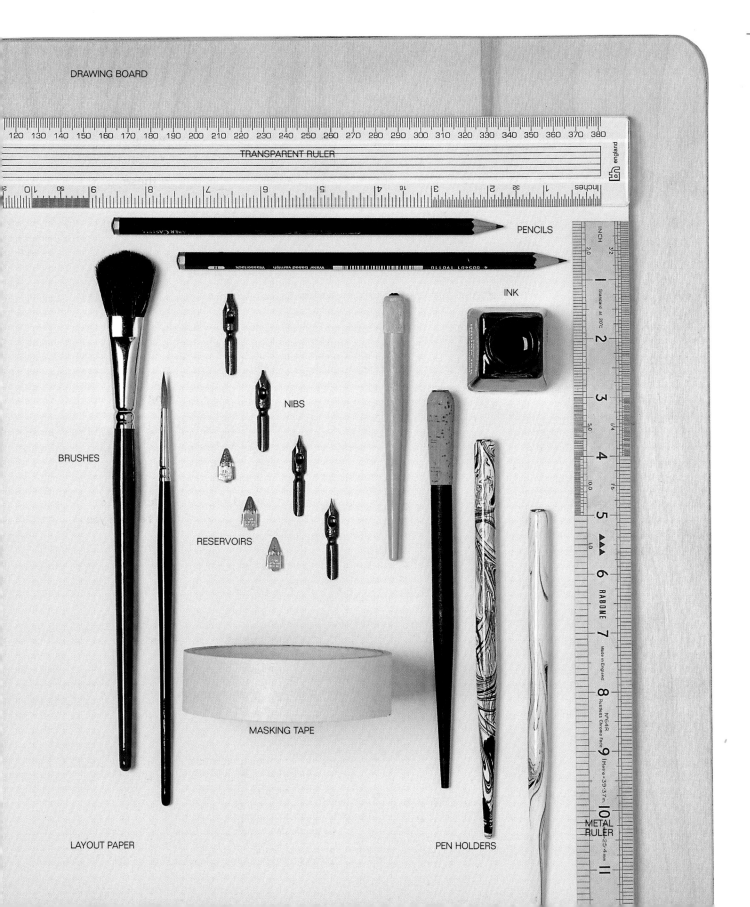

DRAWING BOARD

TRANSPARENT RULER

PENCILS

INK

NIBS

BRUSHES

RESERVOIRS

MASKING TAPE

METAL RULER

LAYOUT PAPER

PEN HOLDERS

CUTTING MAT: This is a special mat made from "self-healing" rubber that does not blunt or damage scalpel or craft knife blades. Thick card is a cheaper, temporary alternative.

KNIFE: A scalpel with disposable blades should be used for trimming out finished work. A pointed blade is best for this, but scalpels have different blades for different applications. Use a craft or Stanley knife for heavy card, as the stronger blades will withstand the extra pressure required without snapping. Both knives are useful for sharpening your pencils to a really sharp point.

PAINT: Designer's gouache is the most commonly used paint for writing with a dip pen. Watercolour paints are used to make background washes (see page 15).

PALETTE: A china palette with a number of small wells can be used for mixing paint. A lidded china palette will stop paints drying out.

REPOSITIONABLE GLUE: Cow gum is a non-permanent glue that is useful for making paste-up layouts since it can be repositioned. Glue sticks and glue tapes are also available with repositionable adhesive.

RULING PEN: This pen can be used to rule neat, straight lines in ink or paint. It can also be used to write with.

SCISSORS: Good, sharp scissors are an alternative to a scalpel for paste-ups, but they won't give an accurate enough line for trimming out finished work.

SET SQUARE: Get an adjustable one if possible – it helps with checking pen angles and ruling lines easily at different angles as well as the normal, right-angle lines.

T-SQUARE: Using one of these makes ruling up writing lines much easier as it hooks over the left-hand edge of the drawing board, allowing you to make an accurate horizontal line.

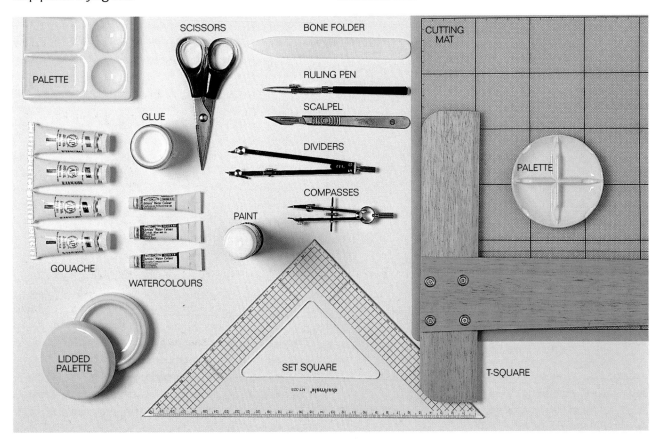

PALETTE
SCISSORS
BONE FOLDER
CUTTING MAT
GLUE
RULING PEN
SCALPEL
DIVIDERS
COMPASSES
PAINT
PALETTE
GOUACHE
WATERCOLOURS
LIDDED PALETTE
SET SQUARE
T-SQUARE

specialist extras

The following tools and materials are needed for specific tasks or processes. Some of these items are available only from specialist shops (see page 79).

ARKANSAS STONE: Used for sharpening nibs (see page 14). A cheaper alternative would be to use 400-grade wet-and-dry paper.

CHINESE INK STICK AND INK STONE: The ink stick is ground into a little distilled water on the ink stone to make your own ink (see pages 14–15).

GUM AMMONIAC: This plant resin is soaked in water to make a size (glue) for gold leaf. It is also available as a ready-made solution.

GUM ARABIC: This substance helps paint flow when the paper surface is slightly shiny or greasy. It can be bought as crystals to be crushed or dissolved in distilled water, or as a ready-made solution.

GUM SANDARACH: In ground form, this material can be dusted over the surface of greasy papers to achieve a crisper line.

MASKING FLUID: A rubber solution that can be applied with a pen or brush (synthetic) as a resist fluid, repelling paint or ink laid over the top of it.

OX GALL LIQUID: Like gum arabic, this substance aids the paint flow from a pen or brush.

POUNCE: This fine powder is used to remove grease from the paper surface.

PVA GLUE: A permanent adhesive that dries clear. Buy an acid-free variety to avoid long-term damage to paper. Mixed with water it makes a gesso for gilding. Can also be used as a varnish.

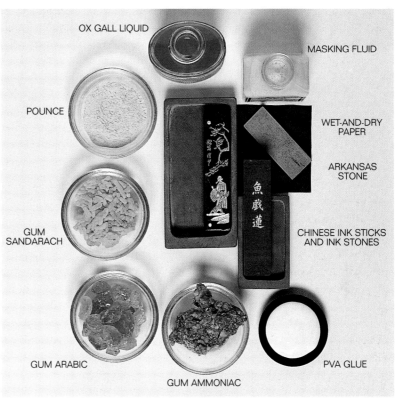

OX GALL LIQUID

MASKING FLUID

POUNCE

WET-AND-DRY PAPER

ARKANSAS STONE

GUM SANDARACH

CHINESE INK STICKS AND INK STONES

GUM ARABIC

GUM AMMONIAC

PVA GLUE

looking after your materials

Taking care of your tools in the following ways will ensure that they continue to produce great results.

Rinse and wipe nibs and reservoirs during and after use, to stop them getting clogged with ink. Agitate the pen to loosen the ink, then dry off the nib and reservoir on a paper towel, but avoid catching loose fibres in the nib tines. Change the water from time to time.

Always wash brushes out thoroughly after use. Rinse first under running warm water, then rub it over a cake of soap and lather gently to loosen any paint or ink. Rinse again in warm water, repeating the soap and rinse stages until the water runs clear. Dry carefully on a paper towel and repoint the bristles. If any hairs stick out, another touch on the soap will help them back in place.

Replace caps and lids on containers to stop evaporation and spillage. A pad of masking tape on the bottom of the bottle is a good way to prevent accidents.

Save your blades by pushing them into a cork or piece of eraser when not in use.

setting up your studio

The set-up of your studio or workspace is essential to your comfort and health, but for the beginner this task need not be expensive or time-consuming. There are just a few basic points to remember.

Commercially made drawing boards are quite expensive, but a sheet of plywood or MDF, 5 mm (about $\frac{1}{4}$ in) thick with the edges sanded smooth makes a good substitute. This can be propped up at an angle against a table and rested on your knee. The angle will depend on how comfortable it is for you and on the work you are doing. Diagrams (A) and (B) show ways of maintaining the board angle.

Pad your board with several sheets of blotting paper or newspaper under a sheet of cartridge paper, secured with masking tape. This will give a more responsive base than the hard board.

You will need a guard sheet of clean, plain paper taped over the bottom half of the board, to protect your work from greasy hands and spills. It keeps the work in place, but allows you to move it easily as necessary.

Slit a cardboard tube lengthways and slip it over the edge of the board to prevent large sheets of paper getting creased. Secure with masking tape.

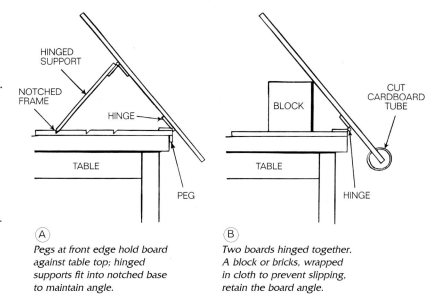

(A)
Pegs at front edge hold board against table top; hinged supports fit into notched base to maintain angle.

(B)
Two boards hinged together. A block or bricks, wrapped in cloth to prevent slipping, retain the board angle.

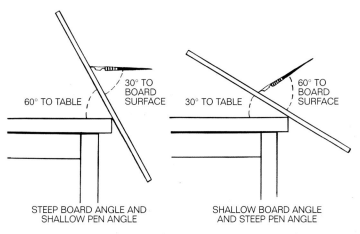

STEEP BOARD ANGLE AND SHALLOW PEN ANGLE

SHALLOW BOARD ANGLE AND STEEP PEN ANGLE

Board angle and penshaft angle should work together for best ink flow. Experiment to find what works best for you.

are you sitting comfortably?

Set your board up in an area with good light to avoid eye strain. Daylight is best, with a north-facing window giving the most even light. If this is not possible, use an adjustable anglepoise lamp with a "blue" bulb, which imitates daylight. Light should come from the left if you are right-handed and vice versa for left-handers. Aim to avoid shadows over the working area, which is important when you are mixing and matching colours.

Make sure the table is large enough to give you room on either side of the board to lay out your pens and other materials.

The chair should support your back and help to keep you sitting up straight. At all costs resist the temptation to lean forwards as you work, this will soon cause back and neck pains. A height adjustable chair is the ideal solution.

the specifics

Most of the materials mentioned here should be available in large art shops. The more obscure items, such as ink sticks and stones, tend to be stocked by specialist retailers, although there are some exceptions. Some of these shops have excellent mail order services, or online shopping facilities. See the stockists and suppliers list on page 79 for more information.

pens

Quills or reeds were the earliest writing tools, but these need special preparation and skilled cutting, so most calligraphers now use metal nibs, which are widely available. Dip pens are the most widely used, and can be fitted with a variety of different shaped nibs, and used with ink or paint.

NIBS FOR DIP PENS: The sort of writing dealt with in this book requires broad-edged nibs. These have writing edges, not points, and make thick and thin strokes naturally without the need for heavy pressure. If you have never used a nib like this before, it may take a little getting used to, but the exercises described later in the book will help you.

Several manufacturers make broad-edged nibs. You are likely to find it easiest to buy nibs as complete sets from the widest (0) to the finest (6) with a pen holder, but they can be obtained singly from specialist suppliers (see page 79). Practically, you need only two or three to begin with, such as a No. $1\frac{1}{2}$ (3 mm/$\frac{1}{8}$ in), a No. 3 (1.5 mm/$\frac{1}{16}$ in) and a No. 4 (1 mm/$\frac{1}{32}$ in), the mid- to larger sizes being slightly easier to control than the fine nibs when you are just beginning.

When buying nibs, scrutinize them carefully. Discard any which are crooked, badly formed or have splayed tines. There are special left-oblique nibs for left-handers. Square-edged nibs are also usable with ink, paint and other writing fluids.

PEN HOLDERS: To use broad-edged nibs, a pen holder which feels comfortable for the size of your hand is essential. They vary from basic round plastic ones which cost very little, to exquisitely crafted wooden ones at the top of the price range. Once you have found a style you like, buy one pen holder for each nib you are likely to use so that you don't have to keep swapping the nibs around, getting inky fingers in the process.

RESERVOIRS FOR DIP PENS: These are very useful devices for holding a small supply of ink on the nib. I prefer the slip-on type, which go under the nib, as I find the ink flows well with this variety. Reservoirs need to slide on snugly enough not to fall off, but not so tightly that the ink is restricted by the squashed tines. The "wings" of a reservoir can be adjusted relatively easily for a good fit (see page 19). Other types of nibs have an over-nib reservoir that holds the ink supply above the slit between the tines, rather than below it. These can be adjusted by bending them upwards to allow more space for the ink.

FOUNTAIN PENS: Calligraphy fountain pen sets are fairly widely available. They are best suited for normal handwriting or for trying out ideas quickly, rather than for finished work. The main drawbacks are the limited range of nib sizes and the fact that you are restricted to using very thin ink in cartridges, and certainly not paint.

AUTOMATIC PENS: These are used for large-scale work, but they also come in a variety of forms to give many different types of line. Load with a brush and they will write well with ink or paint. Putting several colours into one pen can be fun and produces interesting as well as unexpected effects.

nib sharpening

Most nibs will write perfectly well for some time, but you do need to keep them sharp for consistently crisp writing. Follow this procedure with some caution as it is quite as easy to ruin a nib as it is to improve it. Drop a little distilled water onto a sheet of 400-grade wet-and-dry paper (or a fine-grade Arkansas stone) laid on a flat surface. With the nib upper side to the abrasive surface supported by the middle finger, pull the pen to the right, pushing down gently and evenly with your thumb – don't press too hard. Left-handers should reverse the direction of pull. Repeat this motion two or three times (1).

"Write" a figure of eight in the water a couple of times to remove any burrs of metal (2). Blot the nib dry.

Check that both tines of the nib have been sharpened equally by looking at them through a magnifying lens, then try it out on layout paper with a little ink. Take care not to oversharpen, or the nib corners will cut into the paper. Step 2 helps to avoid this but sharp corners can be touched very gently on the abrasive paper or grind stone.

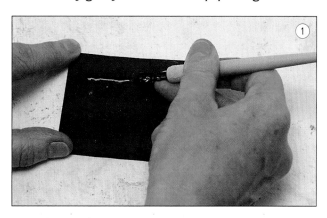

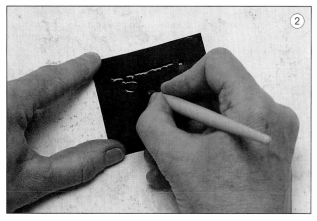

inks

BLACK INKS: Ready-prepared liquid carbon black inks, are the most widely available. Use the non-waterproof kind so that your nibs do not get clogged with the shellac present in waterproof types. The ink should give a fine, clear line and can be thinned with distilled water if necessary. The many different brands vary in composition, so use trial and error to find the one you like best. Ease of flow, density and consistency of colour are the important criteria. Remember that ordinary fountain pen inks are too thin for use with dip pens.

COLOURED INKS: Use these with discretion. Their colours tend to be rather vivid and acidic, which can be rather hard on the eye, and the consistency of coverage and opacity is patchy, but they might just give the effect you want. Check that they are non-waterproof before you buy. You will also need to be very thorough in cleaning pens and particularly brushes after use. For solid colour coverage use gouache paints (see page 15).

CHINESE INK STICK: This is my favourite kind of ink, but it does take a little time to prepare. The ink stick is ground with water on a special stone. Better quality sticks produce blacker inks; those with a matt surface are more reliable for quality than shiny ones.

grinding ink

Choose a large ink stone that gives you room to move the ink stick during grinding. Use an eye dropper to drop a measured quantity of distilled water – following the manufacturer's instructions or using your own recipe – onto the stone and rub the stick on the surface in a rhythmic circular motion (3). Make a note of the quantity of water and grinding time used to enable you to repeat the exercise reliably. I use 10 drops and grind for $2\frac{1}{2}$ minutes.

Test the ink by writing on a scrap of layout paper to check you have the density of black you want. Grind for longer if it is not black enough, or for a shorter time for a paler grey. Transfer the ink to a small screw-top jar. The ink will stay fresh for a little while, but is better ground fresh each time. Stir before use.

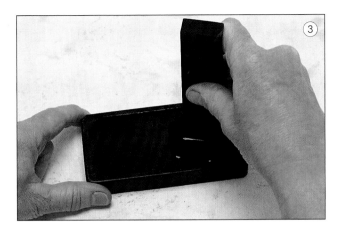

Scrub the stone clean and dry the end of the ink stick to stop it cracking.

The stone will eventually be worn smooth by repeated grinding, but you can refresh the dry surface by rubbing it gently with 400- to 600-grade wet-and-dry paper.

pencils

Buy good quality branded pencils, as the cheaper ones tend to have gritty leads and can be difficult to sharpen adequately. Leads are graded according to hardness. H to 9H are hard, B to 9B are soft, the highest numbers being hardest or softest accordingly.

To rule up for writing, an H or HB sharpened to a good fine point with a scalpel will give you accurate lines. Be careful not to press too hard or you will score the paper. The softer pencils are better for drawing than ruling up, as they give wider, blacker lines and blunt more quickly.

paints

GOUACHE: When you want to use colour in your work, paint is the best option and the type most frequently used by calligraphers is designer's gouache. It gives the best and most consistent results in coverage and opacity, as well as endless possibilities for mixing different colour variations. There is a range of gouache produced specifically for calligraphy, which is very good. On some more absorbent or greasy surfaces, paint will give crisper results than ink, so black gouache is a good standby. Please note that acrylic paints are not suitable for writing with as they dry quickly and will clog your pen.

WATERCOLOURS: These paints give a less opaque finish than gouache or ink for writing, but are very useful for doing transparent colourwashes as backgrounds. Artists' quality will give the best results.

brushes

SABLE BRUSHES: The best quality brushes for use with watercolour and gouache paints are made of Russian red sable. The hair is springy and absorbent, holding colour well. These top quality brushes are best kept for painting, using a No. 3 or 4 for covering larger areas with flat colour. Short-haired brushes (size 000) are perfect for fine details and outlining.

SOFT-HAIRED BRUSHES: These brushes (such as squirrel, ox and goat hair) tend to wear out more quickly and point less reliably than sable. They are perfect, however, for laying washes (large size) or for mixing paint and filling nibs (smaller sizes).

SYNTHETIC BRUSHES: Brushes made with synthetic hair are not as flexible or as sensitive for painting as sable, nor do they hold as much colour. They are reasonably priced and are useful in particular with difficult substances – such as PVA glue, gum ammoniac and masking fluid – that may need to be removed with solvents which would ruin sable brushes. Mixed sable and synthetic brushes are a good all-round compromise.

mixing paint

Mix up a generous quantity of paint in a china palette using distilled water to reproduce the consistency of single cream. You will need plenty of paint to do all the preliminary work as well as the finished piece. This mixture will write very well in a dip pen and give good coverage in areas of brush-painted colour as well.

If the paint dries out in the palette, it is easily reconstituted with a little more water. A lidded china palette will keep the colours moist, or you can cover it with transparent food wrap (cling film) instead.

Keep a different brush for loading each colour onto the pen, and change your water often so that the mixed colours don't become muddy.

Mix the paint the day before you need it. Any excess glycerine will evaporate and the paint becomes less sticky by the time you are ready to use it.

paper

The quality of your finished work will be affected by the type or character of the paper you write on. Your choice will largely depend on the subject matter, the scale of your piece and the effect you want to create with colour and/or texture. Buy the best you can afford. Good quality materials always contribute much to the appeal of the finished article.

- ❑ Small, highly detailed work requires a smooth surface with a slight "tooth" or velvet-like nap which holds the ink or paint, giving crisp edges and fine lines.

- ❑ For larger, less intricate pieces, it is worth experimenting with textured surfaces or handmade papers with petals or grasses incorporated into the sheet.

- ❑ You are likely to find that the written letter will be broken up by heavily textured papers.

- ❑ Soft-surfaced papers, like those for fine printmaking, need care in use because metal nibs catch in the fibres.

- ❑ Shiny surfaces are not ideal, as the nib will skid and ink can make unsightly blobs. However, paint or ink adhesion may be improved (as on other papers which need degreasing) with a light dusting of pounce or ground gum sandarach, brushed off thoroughly before writing.

- ❑ Very absorbent papers are not suitable for calligraphic work using pens, although it may be possible to draw and paint on this type of surface.

Vellum, also known as parchment and made from calf skin, was the traditional surface used for writing before paper was widely and cheaply available. This beautiful material is still used today, but it is expensive and requires special preparation before it can be written on. Good handmade paper is an excellent alternative.

types of paper

HANDMADE PAPER: Comes in individual sheets with four deckle (rough) edges, and is, literally, made by hand.

MACHINE-MADE PAPER: Made on a roller, this paper comes with four cut edges and in a huge variety of colours and textures, not all are suitable for writing on.

MOULD-MADE PAPER: This paper approximates the look of handmade paper at a lower cost. It is made on a roller, so large widths and lengths are available. In sheet form it has two cut and two deckle edges.

surface texture

The surface texture of a sheet of paper is affected mostly by the drying process, but also by the mesh used in the mould.

HOT PRESSED (HP): A smooth surface is made by passing the paper through heated glazing rollers. This refers to watercolour and printing papers.

NOT: Sheets of paper are collected and lightly pressed again, which evens out the texture, although it does retain some character. Generally refers to watercolour papers.

ROUGH: Paper allowed to dry naturally, in particular, watercolour paper, takes on the texture of the mat. Mats are blankets of wool felt in which the pulp is pressed to remove excess water. Best suited to large scale, bold work with brush, reed or automatic pen lettering.

LAID: A pattern of horizontal and vertical lines is impressed onto the surface. The reverse side is flat, rather like a not surface.

WOVE: An even texture made by the woven mesh on both mould and mat. Layout paper falls into this category.

paper sizing

Most papers, especially those most suitable for calligraphy, have size added when the pulp is in the vat. Without size, any ink or paint applied to the surface would sink straight in, as with blotting paper. Some papers are surface-sized, but the size in this case tends to repel ink, making the paper difficult to write on, although adding a drop of ox gall liquid to the ink makes writing easier. Ask the supplier about the sizing before you buy. While not necessarily crucial (unless you need to stretch the paper – soaking will remove all the size from surface-sized types), it will help to know before you start work. Keep a file of samples, with notes about sizing and any necessary preparation required, for future reference.

weights of paper

This is measured in grams per square metre (gsm) or pounds per ream (lb). The smaller the number the lighter the weight. Weight is most important when making manuscript books, because you need to consider the bulk of the folded sheets.

paper grain

If machine-made paper is to be folded to make a book or greetings card, you must first establish the grain direction of the fibres. Without doing this, the book or card will not open properly and it will curl at the edges. To work this out, test fold your paper as the diagram shows. Folding with the grain gives least resistance.

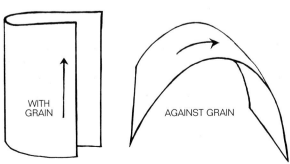

WITH GRAIN

AGAINST GRAIN

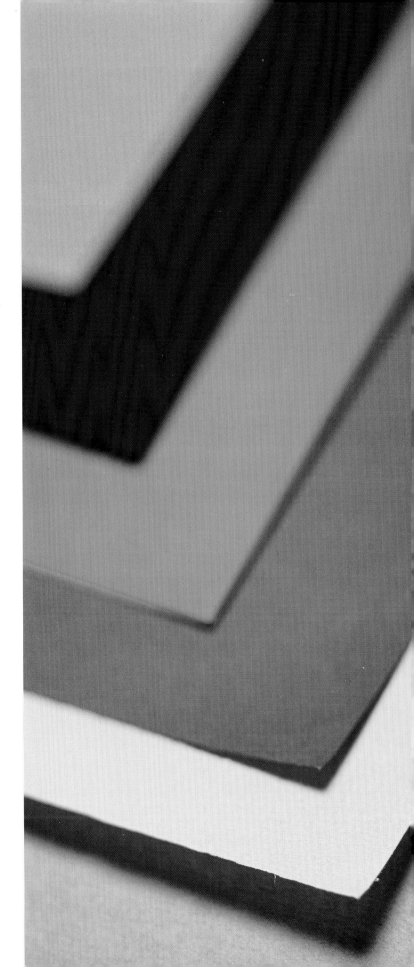

your paper stock

Collect a selection of basic papers, suited to various types of work, but you will always need to have the following close at hand:

LAYOUT PAPER: Buy an A2 pad (420 x 594 mm/ 16½ x 23¼ in) if possible, but anything smaller than A3 (420 x 297 mm/16½ x 11¾ in) is not really economical. More importantly, a smaller pad restricts how you see your work on the paper, and the size of the writing. Layout paper is perfect for practice and roughs; as it is semi-transparent, it is useful for tracing off various stages and refining your designs.

TRACING PAPER: Available in pads or rolls, tracing paper is invaluable for refining designs and lettering as well as transferring the design onto the final paper.

CARTRIDGE PAPER: If of reasonable quality, cartridge paper is useful for all sorts of written or drawn lettering work, though perhaps not always for finished projects.

GLASSINE: For protecting work in progress or as an overlay for finished work. Also used in gilding.

Do not feel restricted to using off-white papers all the time. Art shops stock coloured papers for watercolour or pastel work which are also suitable for calligraphy, but the specialist suppliers offer a much wider choice and will provide you with samples of the types they stock for a fee.

Choose large sheets rather than pads for finished work, and buy enough to allow for making mistakes. You will also need extra on which to try colours out first.

looking after paper

Paper is best stored flat, away from extremes of heat and cold and protected from dust. Ensure your hands are clean before handling paper and hold it carefully in a loose curve so it is less likely to crease – particularly important with very lightweight paper.

If you have to roll paper for storage or transport, roll it loosely with the grain and slip it into a wide cardboard tube. Unroll the paper and lay it flat as soon as possible.

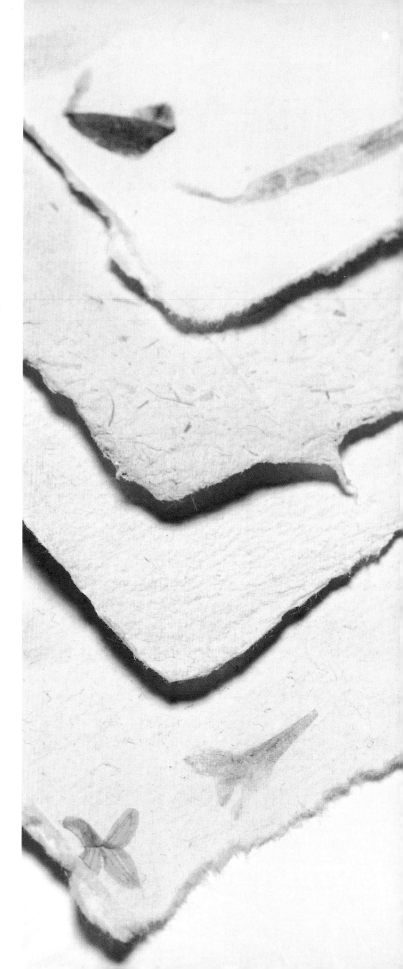

making your mark

In order to make good marks, you need to familiarize yourself with the feel of a broad-edged nib, find out what sort of lines it makes and how the angle of the nib and the amount of pressure you exert will influence those marks.

before you begin

First set up your drawing board at the best, most comfortable angle for you (see page 12).

Some nibs have a greasy coating which can be removed by dipping the nib into boiling water, then into cold water, or by holding the nib in the flame of a match for two to three seconds before dipping it into cold water.

Attach the reservoir and adjust it (1). It needs to be just tight enough to stay in place – too tight and the nib tines will splay, too loose and it will fall off. Always remove and clean the reservoir after use or it will go rusty.

Dip a brush into the ink or paint and apply it to the underside of the nib, feeding it between the nib and reservoir (2). Dipping your nib straight into the ink bottle results in blobs and inky fingers, as the ink flow is not under control. Doing it this way should result in nice crisp strokes.

Wash and dry the nib regularly as you work to stop the nib from clogging. Use a paper towel or rag that doesn't shed fibres, or you could get fuzzy edges. Repeat the process when you have finished writing.

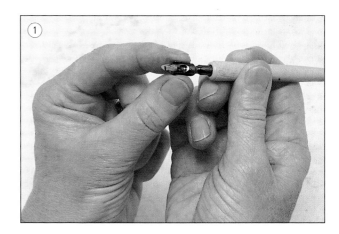

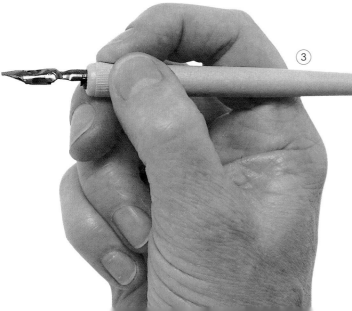

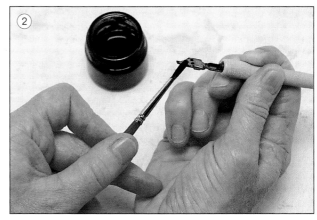

Hold your pen comfortably between thumb and forefinger, sloping it back towards your hand (3). Your arm should be relaxed and supported from elbow to wrist on the drawing board so that hand, wrist and fingers can move freely, enabling you to control the pen more easily.

the first stroke

The nib should make perfect contact on the paper (4), with both tines touching the surface under light, but even pressure. Too much pressure will make the nib splay, give a distorted stroke, and may damage it and the nib. If this is a problem, try holding a bone folder in your other hand. This not only holds the paper in place and keeps your fingers off the surface, it also takes away the pressure from your writing hand. Remember, broad-edged nibs make thick and thin strokes naturally without excess pressure.

If the nib does not write first time, you will need to make side to side movements – on scrap paper – to make the ink flow from the nib properly. If it still doesn't write: check that the reservoir is not too tight, restricting the ink flow; dust the paper, which may be greasy, with powdered gum sandarach, clean it off and have a guard sheet under your hand; or add a little distilled water to the ink or paint which may be too thick to flow well, and test it again. If your first marks are a bit ragged, it could be due to uneven pressure on one side of the nib or a rough surfaced paper making the line break up. The latter can be exploited to good effect sometimes, but not at the beginning.

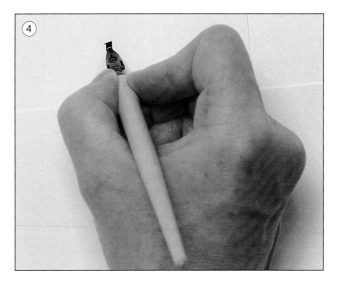

basic pen strokes

First, draw some pencil lines on a sheet of layout paper, then load your nib – start with a large size such as a No. 1½. Holding the pen at an angle of 30° (A) to the writing line, write the strokes shown (B), repeating them at 45° (C and D).

These are the basic building blocks of letters. Try some basic pen strokes using angles of 30°, 45° and 90° (E),

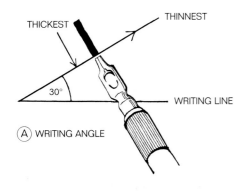

THICKEST THINNEST

30°

WRITING LINE

(A) WRITING ANGLE

(B) BASIC STROKES AT 30° PEN ANGLE
Arrows show direction of strokes.

(C) BASIC STROKES AT 45° PEN ANGLE

30° ROUNDED   45° ROUNDED   30° POINTED   45° POINTED   30° JOINED   45° JOINED   i.e. ARCHES – 30°   45°

(D) VERTICALS AND SERIFS
Combine different strokes to make more complex patterns. Use different nib-widths for more variations.

 30° 45° 90° (E) BASIC PEN STROKES
The effect of different pen angles.

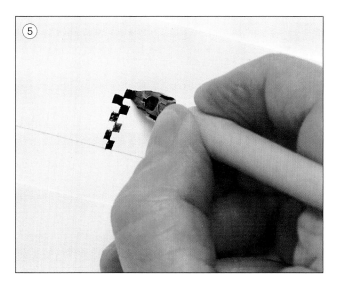

Curves, arches and diagonal lines are reasonably easy to achieve successfully, verticals take a little more practice – work steadily until you can write longish lines without wobbling.

working out the letter height

Before you start to write actual letters, you need to know how to work out the body height, or "x"-height – that is, with no ascenders or descenders – of these letters. Historically, each "style" evolved to a particular size, usually one most suited to the writing out of texts in books, but any style can be enlarged or reduced in proportion to the size of nib you are going to use, by making a nib-width scale (5).

grouping them together according to the angles used, and observe how the resulting patterns differ from each other. The different letter styles all have their own rhythm and practising these strokes and patterns will help you to get the feel of this. Try developing them into zigzags, diamonds, boxes, the possibilities are endless (F and G).

Write the strokes close together, then do them again with wider spacing, concentrating on keeping the spacing even each time, whether it is open or tight (D).

Draw a pencil baseline on some scrap paper, then mark up a series of horizontal steps like a ladder to the required number (you'll find this given on each exemplar page). Do this carefully, the strokes should be joined accurately top and bottom to give a true size. When all the marks have been made, draw in a line across the top. Calculate the height of capitals, ascenders and descenders and even line spacing in the same way.

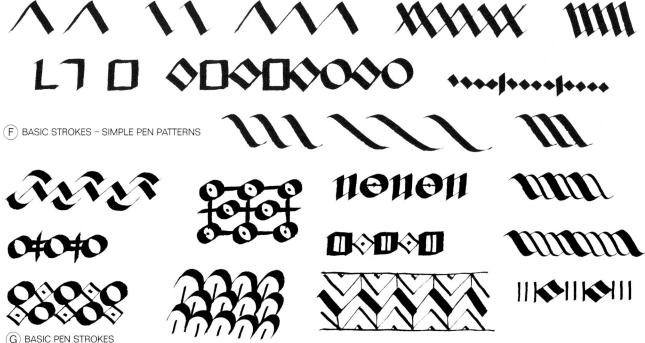

(F) BASIC STROKES – SIMPLE PEN PATTERNS

(G) BASIC PEN STROKES
Combine different strokes to make more complex patterns. Use different nib-widths for more variations.

ruling up

You can transfer these marks for letter height to paper to give a series of writing lines in two ways. Either set a pair of dividers to the correct measurement and "walk" them down the page, or make a paper ruler (H) and tick off the marked spaces with a sharp pencil before ruling up.

   If you don't have a T-square, make the first mark of your scale a measured distance from the top edge at both sides of the paper. Continue the marks down both sides, taking care to be accurate, then rule lines across joining the marks (I).

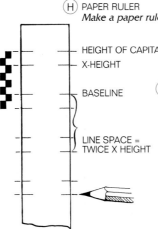

(H) PAPER RULER
Make a paper ruler, marking off from the ladder scale.

HEIGHT OF CAPITAL
X-HEIGHT

BASELINE

LINE SPACE = TWICE X HEIGHT

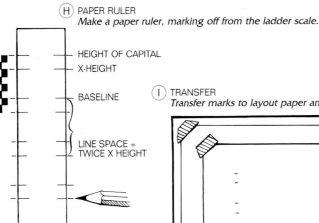

(I) TRANSFER
Transfer marks to layout paper and rule up, joining the pencil marks.

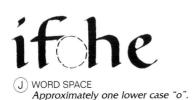

(J) WORD SPACE
Approximately one lower case "o".

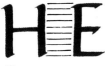

(K) STRAIGHT LETTERS
Furthest apart.

(L) STRAIGHT AND CURVED LETTERS
Have less space between them.

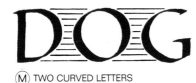

(M) TWO CURVED LETTERS
Closer still.

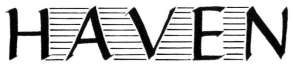

(N) COUNTERS
Spacing between letters should look even and equal to the space inside the letters (counters).

principles of spacing

Good spacing is crucial to the success of your lettering. If it is poor, legibility will suffer and the reader's interest will be lost. Here are the basic guidelines:

   A word space (J) should be equal to approximately one lower case "o". Two straight letters together (K) are furthest apart, there should be slightly less space between a straight letter and a curved one (L) and two curved letters together (M) have the least space between them. What you are actually doing is making visual compensation for the visible space within the letters (counters) (N). Mechanical spacing doesn't really work, it should look even.

analyzing letterforms

You have looked at how to get your pen ready to write, tried some strokes and got used to the feel of the pen. Now is the time to look at some examples of different hands which will be used in the projects later in the book.

   Each one has its own characteristics which can be analyzed using a formula devised by the English calligrapher Edward Johnston, initially to help him, and later his students, to understand the principles of good lettering. The criteria work for any script, ancient or modern.

- **THE WEIGHT** of the letter: that is, the thickness of the heaviest stroke. This gives you the unit of measurement for judging letter height.
- **THE ANGLE** of the pen to the writing line. Use a sharp pencil and tracing paper to mark the angles, then use a protractor to check them. Note where angles may be steeper or flatter to avoid inconsistencies in weight.
- **THE FORM** of the letter. This is dictated by the pen angle, but look at the letters "o" and "a", to give a sense of the form (round, oval or angular). Note how the serifs are made (see page 25).
- **THE NUMBER OF STROKES** needed to make each letter. Look at where the pen lifts occur – after the "pull" strokes and at the ends of serifs.
- **THE ORDER OF STROKES.** This follows naturally from left to right and top to bottom.
- **THE DIRECTION OF STROKES.** Do they go up or down or diagonally? Broad-edged nibs write best pulled towards you, pushed away the ink may sputter.
- **THE SPEED OF WRITING.** Look for joins between letters and strokes which overrun.

make your writing practice effective

- Be systematic. Study the exemplars one at a time and stick with it for a while. It is important to be familiar with and understand the structure of the script before you begin to write, so follow the analytical principles given and look carefully at the shapes. It's easy to copy the given exemplars, they give you the means to achieve an end (your completed project), but knowing how to analyze the letterforms will inform your writing.
- You could make your first efforts with double pencils, which make the letter structure even clearer. Bind two pencils (HB) together with masking tape and write with them in the same way as with a pen (6).
- Aim to write how you know it should look, not how you think it should.
- Start with capitals, they are easier to cope with, but move on to writing minuscules as soon as your confidence allows.

writing with paint

- *Load your pen as already described for ink (see page 19) and adjust the drawing board to a shallower angle, which stops colour settling to the bottom of the letters (see page 12).*
- *Stirring the paint often keeps the pigments from separating.*
- *Clean the nib frequently or the paint will dry and clog the nib.*
- *Try writing without a reservoir on the nib. This can be easier, but it does require more frequent and more careful loading of the nib. Practise this technique on spare paper, to gain confidence before tackling a finished piece.*
- *Solve problems with uneven paint flow by adding a drop or two of ox gall or gum arabic liquids to the mix. Ox gall improves paint adhesion as well as flow; gum arabic has similar properties, but adds an extra gloss to the colour when dry.*
- *If the paint is inclined to be sticky, put gum arabic in the mixing water rather than in the paint mix.*
- *Always use clean water for mixing and keep a separate jar of water for rinsing out your brushes.*

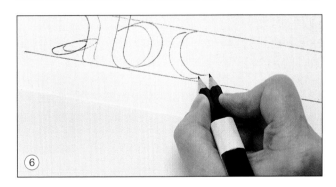

(6)

- Keep writing until you can form the letters without having to refer to the original model.
- Write words, phrases and sentences. This is much more helpful than just repeating alphabets *ad nauseam.* Aim to write legible letters fluently, with appropriate letter, word and line spacing.

personal style

Let your own style grow gradually. It's tempting to copy exciting pieces of modern calligraphy without knowing the thought processes behind them. If you do copy something, use the letter analysis formula to try and understand what makes it work. Try to avoid any mannerisms; incorporating these will not help with your own personal style. You really don't need gimmicks to bring a sense of style to your work, just study the seven constants in Edward Johnston's formula.

The following exemplars and their variations are not exhaustive.
Use them as a springboard from which to jump into your own experiments.

ROMANCAPITALS

Skeleton or monoline capitals show the geometrical construction and the relative proportions of these letters. They are the foundation of the capitals on the opposite page. The basic grid for these letters is a circle within a square. One-eighth of the square is cut off at each side, leaving a rectangle which visually is equal to the area of the circle.

the letters fall into family groups:

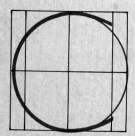

round letters **O C D G Q**

Based on the circle, with straight sides relating to the rectangle. O and Q should curve very slightly through the writing lines top and bottom. C and G have the top stroke slightly flattened.

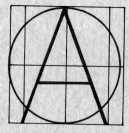

rectangular letters **A H N U V X Y Z**

Letters with straight sides and diagonals. The cross bar of H is slightly above the centre, on A it is just below the centre.

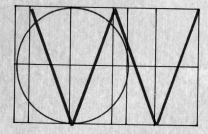

extra wide letters **M W**

W is made up of two Vs side by side (i.e. two rectangles). M is the full width of the square at its base, although strokes 1 and 4 begin on the edges of the rectangle.

narrow letters 1) **B E F K L P R** 2) **S J**

Use half-width squares for narrow letters. The curves are still based on circles. The cross bar of F is lower than that of E to balance the white space. The bottom cross bars of E and L are slightly longer than the upper ones.

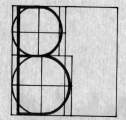 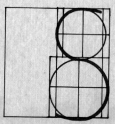

ABCDEFGHI
JKLMNOPQR
STUVWXYZ

Try writing these letters with a pencil first between lines ruled 25 mm (1 in) apart and then use double pencils (see page 23). Skeleton letters can be used in their own right, not just as an exercise, so follow up the pencil letters using a fine nib. To put "flesh" on your skeleton letters, write them again with double pencils (see page 23).

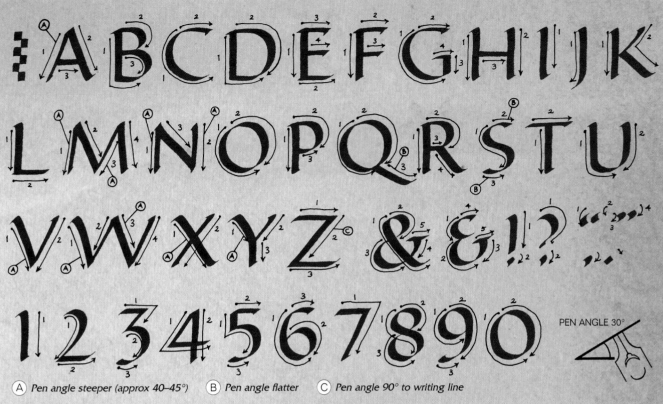

Ⓐ Pen angle steeper (approx 40–45°)   Ⓑ Pen angle flatter   Ⓒ Pen angle 90° to writing line

These letters are usually used in a formal way, as they were originally in stone inscriptions or as important headings in manuscripts and books.

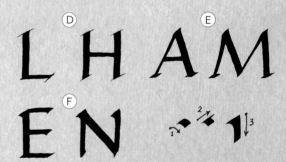

how to make serifs

In the example above, the serifs are really small ticks made as the pen is lifted off the paper. These can be varied in three ways: (D) fine lines made with the pen at 90° to the writing line, (E) slab serifs written at approximately 30° (the same as the rest of the letter), (F) built up with three strokes to make a triangular shape. This requires some care to make the strokes blend into each other.

THE QUICK BROWN FOX JUMPS OVER THE LAZY DOG

spacing

Space the letters to look equal, with the word space slightly less than O. If the letter spacing is too tight, dark patches will appear and the Os will look like holes. If too open, the letters will not connect as words. The line space is the same as the height of the letters.

FOUNDATIONHAND

Edward Johnston chose an English 'Caroline' minuscule (from the manuscript *Harley 2904* in the British Library) for his foundational hand, which he developed as a basic round hand for formal writing. The example given here owes much to those early researches, but is adapted for modern use and has smaller serifs. The foundation hand is a useful hand for formal work and Roman capitals are usually used with these lower case letters. It is based on a circle within a square, where the rectangle equals the area of the circle.

the letters fall into family groups:

round letters **b c d e o p**
Bottom curve of p, top curves of d and q are flattened.

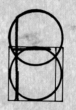

straight letters **f i j l t**
Top curve of f is flattened and cross bar is below x-height. Cross bar of t is on x-height line.

arched letters **a h m n r u**
m is twice the width of n. u follows the lower part of o.

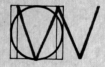

diagonal letter strokes **k v w x y z**
w is twice the width of v. Top of x is inside the rectangle, bottom is outside. Bottom stroke of z is slightly wider than the rectangle.

ungrouped **s g**
Top of g is smaller than o, bottom half is wider, a flattened oval.

relative proportions of letters

Lower case letters are $\frac{2}{3}$ height of the capital.
Ascenders and descenders are $\frac{2}{3}$ height of the capital.

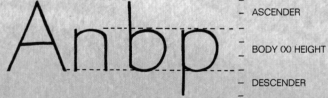

– ASCENDER

– BODY (X) HEIGHT

– DESCENDER

variations in letter weight

At the standard 4 nib widths x-height for any nib, the letter weight can be altered by using a thinner or thicker nib, using the same standard x-height. This is useful when you start to design pieces of work.

STANDARD HEIGHT USING A NO. 2 NIB

WRITTEN WITH A NO. 5 NIB

WRITTEN WITH A NO. 1 NIB

abcdefghijklmnopq
rstuv
wxyz

Practice writing these skeleton letters with a pencil to get used to the shapes they make. When you are confident of the forms in pencil, rule up and write out the alphabet as shown opposite using pen and ink.

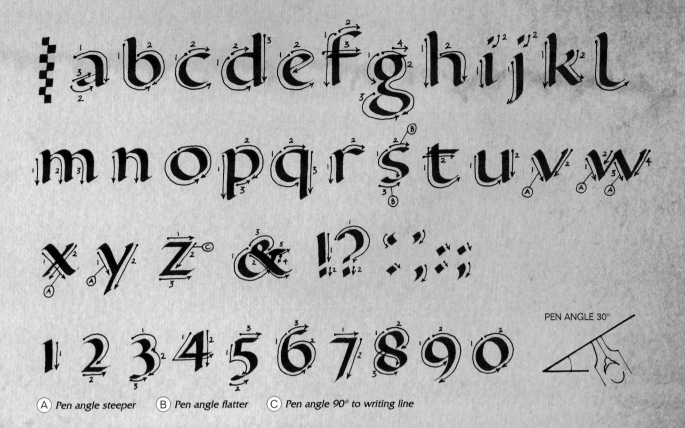

A Pen angle steeper   B Pen angle flatter   C Pen angle 90° to writing line

spacing

Space the letters so that the white space within and between them looks even.
Word space is slightly less than o. Line space is twice the x-height.

The quick brown fox

jumps over the lazy dog

modifications to joins

To improve the appearance of even letter spacing, the first letters are reduced slightly in width.

ea fl ff la ri ry tt

ITALICS

The understanding of the structure of Roman capitals will help when looking at italic capitals, but here the form is oval, not circular. The letter width is two thirds of the height, which alters the relative proportion of all the letters. Look at the internal spaces as well as the overall letter width. This hand is generally used for informal work, although the upright italic has a classic elegance.

lower case letters: related forms

a is the key letter, made up of three strokes. 2 is flattened, 3 is parallel to 1. Most lower case letters follow this form, but fall into rough groups according to the direction of the first stroke. The rhythm of writing the strokes is important. All upstrokes are pushed and the arches spring out from mid-stem.

anti-clockwise, pointed base **a d g q u**

clockwise, arched letters **b h m n p r**

rounded base **c e f o s t**
(f can extend below the baseline)

diagonal letters **i j k v w z y z**

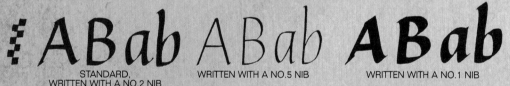

related spaces and position of cross bars

Spaces between arch and stem at the top of letters relates to those at the base. Cross bars hang from the x-height line. The top curve of s relates to that of f.

variation in letter weight

As described on page 22, if you establish the standard capital and x-height for any given nib, you can vary letter weight by writing at the same height with either thinner or thicker nibs.

ABab
STANDARD,
WRITTEN WITH A NO.2 NIB

ABab
WRITTEN WITH A NO.5 NIB

ABab
WRITTEN WITH A NO.1 NIB

flourished capitals

Italic's cursive nature lends itself to flourishes and they are fun to do. Make them as an extension of part of the letter, usually from the thin rather than the thick stroke, though there are exceptions. They should look natural and not disguise the letter shape. Practise them in pencil first to see how they work. The pen-written ones should retain the vitality of your practice letters. Flourishes on D are similar to those for B. On lower case letters, flourishes spring from ascenders and descenders, although some letters can be extended at the end of a line to help balance centred layouts, or even to make a decorative feature at the end of a piece.

ABCDEFGHIJK

LMNOPQRSTU

VWXYZ &&!?

PEN ANGLE 45°

abcdefghijklmn

opqrstuvwxyz

1234567890

spacing

Space capitals visually. Line space is the same as the height of the capitals. Lower case letters need generous interlinear spacing because of the tall ascenders and descenders – twice the x-height as a minimum. Start with generous letter spacing too, then practise closer spacing, adding joins for a more cursive, informal feel.

The quick brown fox jumps over the lazy dog

VERSALS

Versals were originally used as initial letters of verses, as the name suggests, in bibles and other religious books. They provide an effective contrast to most scripts written with broad-edged nibs, but can also be used in their own right as blocks of text. The skeleton capitals on page 24 will help with proportions. The form is round, based on O, although the inside shape of O is quite oval. Most often used in a formal way, in modernized form, they can also be used effectively in informal designs.

letter construction

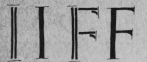

STRAIGHT LETTERS
Outer strokes curve slightly inwards at the centre. Serifs are added last.

CURVED LETTERS
Make inner strokes first. Curved outer strokes start flatter.

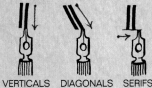

DIAGONALS
In each category, the third stroke fills in the gap created by the outer two.

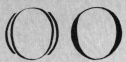

direction and angles of pen movement in letter construction

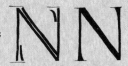

VERTICALS   DIAGONALS   SERIFS   SERIFS   HORIZONTALS

family groups

round **O C D G O Q** relate to O (strokes 2 & 5 on C, 2 on G are flattened)

P R B bowls relate to O. Width of curves needs to be slightly wider than normal stems, to look equal.

S inner curves (strokes 2 & 3) are rounded

diagonal **A M N V W X Y Z**

straight stem **E F H I J L T U**

letter height

Twenty-four nib-widths or eight times the stem width of three strokes. The simplest method is to measure three nib-widths and multiply that by eight.

Practise writing with confidence to avoid wobbles! Learn the shapes so that you can visualize them before you write. An alternative is to draw them in pencil first and fill in with paint and brush, though the end result will differ slightly from pen-written letters. Don't overload the brush otherwise the serifs will not be as fine as they should.

THE QUICK BROWN
FOX JUMPS OVER
THE LAZY DOG

spacing

Space visually, as with Roman capitals. Word space is approximately the inner space of O and the line space is the same as the height of the capitals.

Rule up and write versals between two pencil lines to begin with, but as you gain in confidence and can keep the height even, try to write without the top line.

31

VERSALS

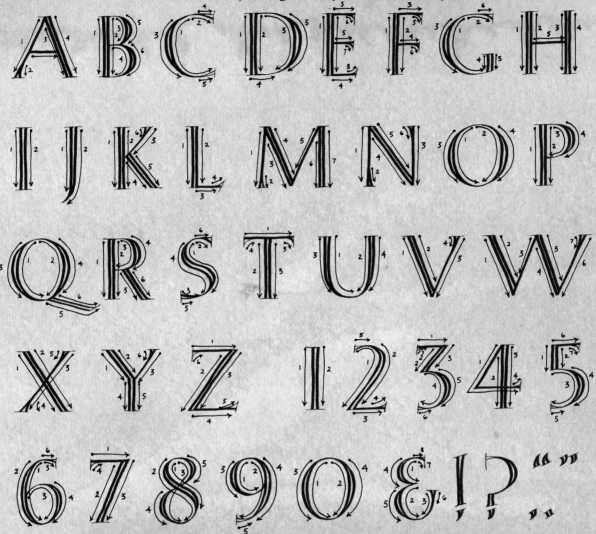

lombardic versals

These generously proportioned letters were common in medieval manuscripts from the 13th–15th centuries. Often highly decorated or on decorative backgrounds, they relate more closely to uncials (see page 6) than to Roman capitals.

variations

Experiment with the letter weight using different nib-widths at the same height: thicker nibs for heavier weight, thinner nibs for light weight letters. Modern versals without serifs can be written upright or slightly slanted. With the latter, as the O becomes more oval than round, the weight of the letter shifts.

practice
projects

The following projects will help further your experience of using broad-edged nibs, as well as exploring the contrasts that can be made by using different nib sizes.

alphabet broadsheet

This project explores how the "colour" of lettering can be varied even in black, by using the same hand but written in different weights and sizes. This idea can be used in the writing out of prose or poetry to add interest and emphasis. Assess the quality of the letterforms as you write so you can improve as you go on.

specific materials

Essential equipment (see pages 8–9)
Dip pen and nibs, Nos $1\frac{1}{2}$, $2\frac{1}{2}$ and 4
Repositionable glue
Cartridge paper

1 Work out the letter height for Roman capitals by making nib-width ladder scales for the three nibs you are going to use (see pages 24–25). Rule up pencil lines on layout paper and write out each alphabet in black ink at the correct height.

2 Rule up more lines on a fresh sheet of layout paper. This time use the smallest nib, No. 4, to write an alphabet at the largest height, the largest nib, No. $1\frac{1}{2}$, at the intermediate height and the middle nib, No. $2\frac{1}{2}$ at the smallest size. You will find writing large letters with a fine nib quite tricky – it takes some practice and a lot of control. Observe the difference in the character of the letters between the two sets of alphabets (1).

3 Cut up the alphabets into strips. Using groups of letters of differing weights, play around with the arrangement until you find one which makes an interesting shape and looks balanced (2). I have used a roughly centred format with quite tight line spacing.

4 Tack the strips of letters in position using repositionable glue, keeping the lines as straight as possible. This new sheet is known as a paste-up. Lay a sheet of tracing paper over the paste-up to assess the effect without the distraction of stuck-down patch marks.

5 Rule up a fresh sheet of layout paper (following your paste-up layout) making any minor adjustments to the position of the letters. Lay this over your paste-up and write, copying from the layout underneath.

6 Rule up a sheet of cartridge paper. Write it out again as a finished piece, making the best letterforms you possibly can.

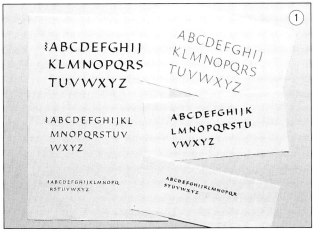

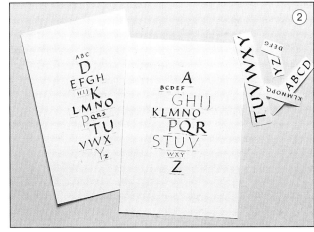

words as
patterns

Writing words, particularly in italics which have such bounce and vitality, can help to establish rhythm in your work. This exercise should also help to develop your eye for good letter shapes, letter spacing, where ligatures (joins) can sensibly be made between letters, as well as the pattern possibilities. Choose a few words on a theme (such as musical terms or names of garden herbs) and make your first attempts just in black ink, then turn to colour for some interesting effects.

specific materials

Essential equipment (see page 8)
Dip pen and nib, No. 1
Repositionable glue
Gouache in two or three toning or contrasting colours
    (such as scarlet lake, cadmium yellow and burnt sienna)
Brushes and palette for mixing gouache
Cartridge paper

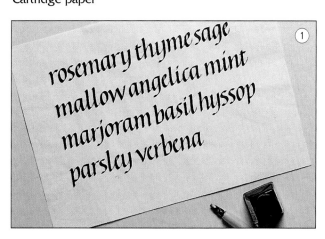

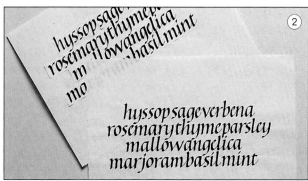

1 Using the No. 1 nib, make a nib-width ladder to establish the correct x-height for the italic hand (see pages 28–29). Rule up a series of writing lines on layout paper at normal line spacing.

2 Following your chosen theme, write out the group of words in black ink, without word spaces, in a different order on each of the lines and varying the starting position each time (1).

3 Cut up the words (or photocopies of them) and experiment with combinations of lines and line spacing, deciding how tight this can be before you have to tuck ascenders or descenders into convenient gaps. Try turning words upside down like a mirror image.

4 Tack down one or more variations to make a paste-up and lay tracing paper over the paste-up to disguise the stuck-down patches.

5 Rule up a fresh sheet of layout paper following your paste-up layout. Lay this over your paste-up and write, copying from the layout underneath (2).

6 Repeat the exercise in colour (see page 15 for how to mix gouache for writing). Use separate brushes to apply each of the colours you use to the nib.

7 When you are happy with it, rule up a sheet of cartridge paper: start by transferring all the relevant marks by using a paper ruler or dividers (see page 22). Write it out again as a finished piece.

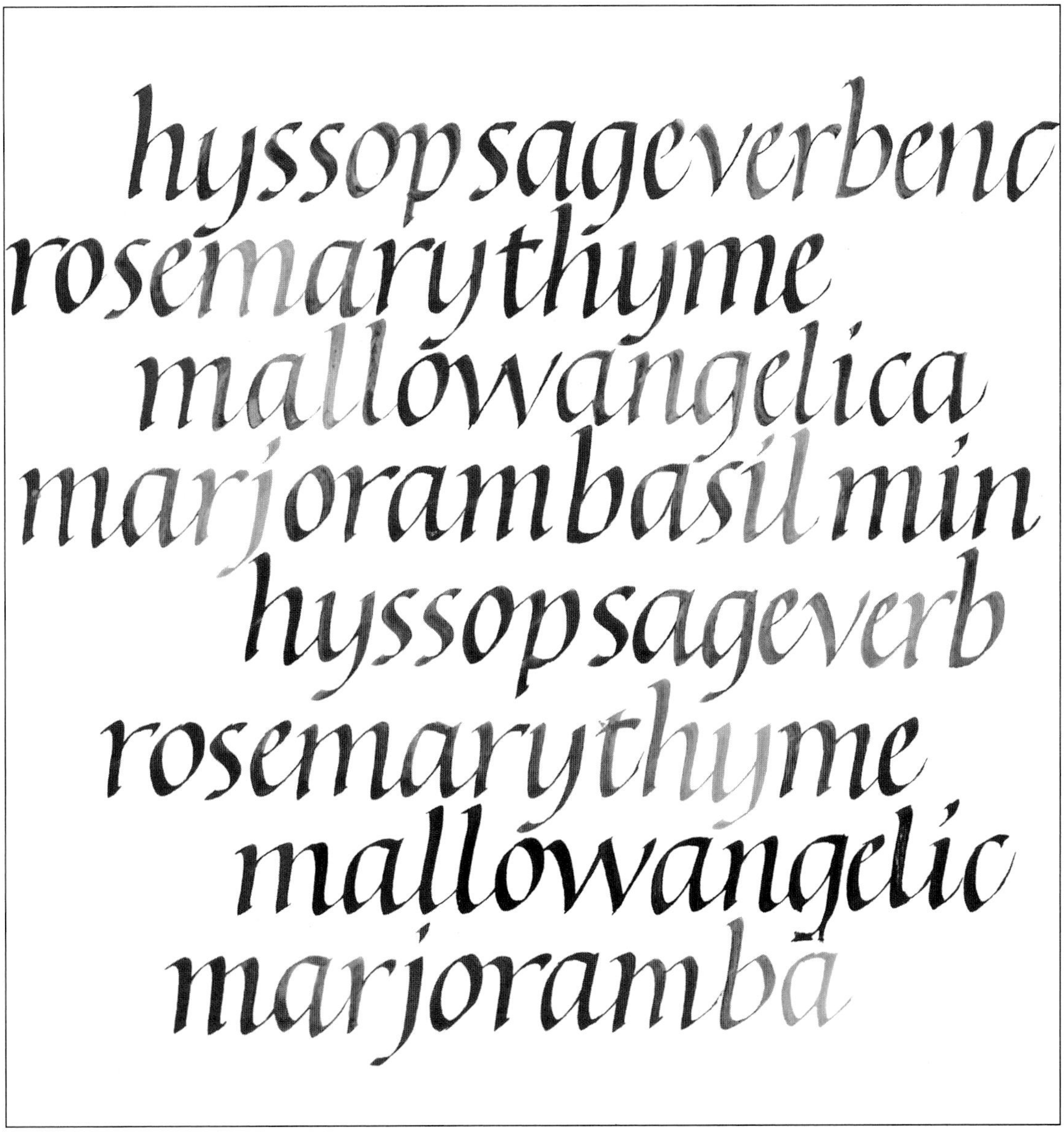

hyssopsageverbenc
rosemarythyme
mallowangelica
marjorambasil min
hyssopsageverb
rosemarythyme
mallowangelic
marjoramba

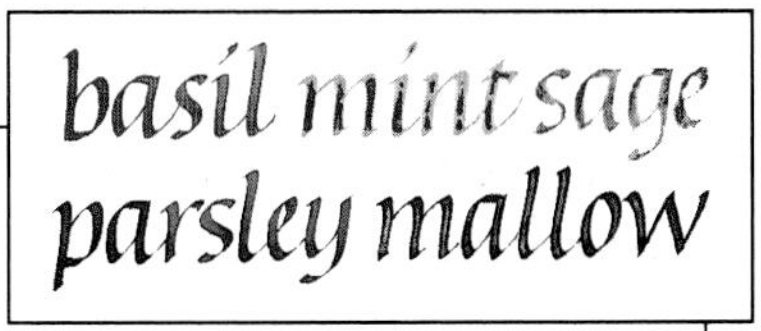

basil mint sage
parsley mallow

mallowangelicasage
sageangelicamallow

Choose contrasting colours like red and yellow or blue and yellow. Write a letter or two in the first colour, then feed in a little of the second and continue to alternate the colours as you write. Wash the nib out and start afresh fairly frequently to preserve the clarity of the colours.

Do all the writing in one colour, but while the paint is still wet, drop in blobs of the second colour, so that the two run into each other (above right). This works best when the base colour is lighter than that dropped in. Alternatively, write the words in plain water and drop colour in before the water dries out (below right).

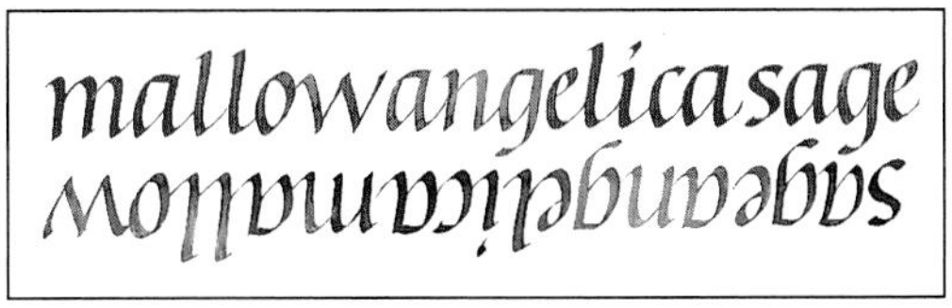

colour variations

design skills

As soon as you have become familiar with the letterforms in the exemplars, you'll be keen to exploit your new skills and make something – a greetings card perhaps, or a menu for a dinner party. The next step is to understand how the design and general concept of a finished piece will affect it. Develop your awareness by looking at everyday things like notices and book covers, and particularly at the work of well-known calligraphers. Consider what constitutes formality or informality and how the size, weight and colour of the letters can focus the reader's attention.

sort out your ideas

Before you start a design, there are a few simple questions to ask yourself, which will help you to organize the elements you want to include. Most of the projects in this book use only small amounts of text, but you need to have these principles in mind, even for very simple pieces.

❑ Who or what is the piece for?
❑ How big do you want the piece to be? This will tend to dictate the size of letters you can use.

❑ Is it a formal or informal piece? The answer might help with the next question.
❑ What letterforms shall I use?
❑ What are the most and the least important elements involved? Logically, the most important needs to be most prominent.
❑ How can I arrange the elements in the space for best effect? The white space around the words is important too, so consider the margins as part of the design.
❑ Will colour play a part in the design, and if so, which colour(s)? The mood or purpose of the piece should help you here.
❑ What materials shall I use? Coloured paper, paint, ink?
❑ Do I want to include any decorative elements and if so, what sort?

Once you have asked yourself the above questions, think about the following concepts:

FORMAT: This principle relates to the second question. The length of lines of the prose or poetry will be a deciding factor in the shape of your finished piece – square, rectangular, vertical or horizontal. Follow the natural pauses, such as ends of phrases and punctuation marks for the line breaks, to keep both the rhythm and sense of the language clear.

SPACING: From the practice projects on pages 32–35, you will have gained an appreciation of how line, word

transferring designs

*O*rdinary carbon paper is fairly greasy and the marks it makes cannot be erased easily, so it is not really suitable for transferring decorative motifs onto finished work. Instead, here are two easy methods you could try.

The first technique works best if the original is on thin tracing paper. Turn over the sheet with the design on it and scribble over the back of all the lines with a 4B or 6B pencil to give a good carbon base. Position the drawing face up in the correct position on the finished piece and, holding it securely in place, use a 6H pencil to redraw over the design. Press down just hard enough to transfer the design without indenting the surface.

To make your own reusable carbon paper, cover a small sheet of thin tracing paper with a thickly scribbled, even layer of carbon from a 6B pencil. Rub it in with your finger to get good adhesion and dust off any surplus. Alternatively, dab Armenian bole held in a thin muslin pouch over a small sheet of tissue paper to give a thick, even layer. Rub it in and dust off the surplus. Use either type as you would normal carbon paper, but any superfluous lines may be removed carefully after painting or writing using a soft eraser.

CONTRAST IN SIZE

TWINKLE
TWINKLE
LITTLE STAR
HOW I WONDER
WHAT
YOU ARE!

CONTRAST IN FORM

twinkle
twinkle
littlestar

how
I wonder
what
you are!

CONTRAST IN WEIGHT

TWINKLE
TWINKLE
LITTLE
STAR
HOW I
WONDER
WHAT
YOU ARE!

CONTRAST IN TEXTURE

TWINKLE
TWINKLE
LITTLE
STAR
HOW I
WONDER
WHAT
YOU
ARE!

UP ABOVE
THE WORLD
SO HIGH
LIKE A
DIAMOND
IN THE
SKY

CONTRAST IN DIRECTION OF WRITING

TWINKLE   TWINKLE   LITTLE STAR   HOW I WONDER   WHAT YOU ARE!

twinkletwinkle
littlestar

TWINKLE   TWINKLE

UP·ABOVE   THE·SKY   SO·HIGH   LIKE   A·DIAMOND   IN·THE·SKY

CONTRAST IN COLOUR

TWINKLE
TWINKLE
LITTLE
STAR
HOW I
WONDER
WHAT
YOU ARE!

and letter spacing affect the visual texture of a finished piece. Use modified spacing, increasing or decreasing space, to add emphasis.

VARIETY: This concept is essential to gaining and then retaining interest. If you are working with more than just a few words, alter the height and/or weight of the text where appropriate by changing the nib size. Colour also brings variety.

EMPHASIS: This principle relates directly to the fifth question. Think about how you could use the size, weight and colour of the lettering to pick out the most important words.

Look at the examples above which illustrate how many different ways there are to introduce contrast into your work, then try them out for yourself using a favourite poem or piece of prose.

planning the finished work

The next stage is planning your finished work. The planning stage is important for any size of project, so don't be tempted to leave it out. It will enable you to sort out your ideas, reject those that don't work, improve on those that do, as well as tuning up the quality of your writing as you go through the process. By the time you are ready to transfer the design onto good paper, you should be reasonably confident of success.

MAKE THUMBNAIL SKETCHES: See below for possible permutations. Sketch your ideas in pencil at a small size on layout paper. See how they look as you alter the position of the elements or vary the weight of the letters by scribbling blacker lines. Try to develop a flexible attitude and play around with all the possibilities until you find a solution that works best for you and will give you promising results.

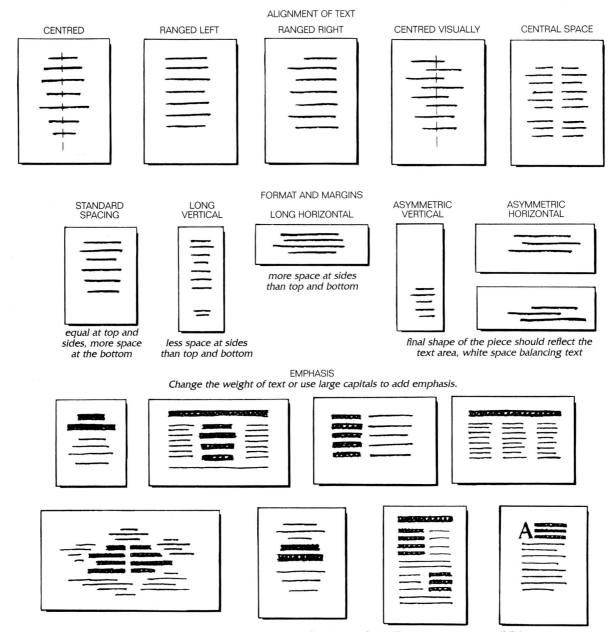

ALIGNMENT OF TEXT

CENTRED RANGED LEFT RANGED RIGHT CENTRED VISUALLY CENTRAL SPACE

FORMAT AND MARGINS

STANDARD SPACING — LONG VERTICAL — LONG HORIZONTAL — ASYMMETRIC VERTICAL — ASYMMETRIC HORIZONTAL

more space at sides than top and bottom

equal at top and sides, more space at the bottom

less space at sides than top and bottom

final shape of the piece should reflect the text area, white space balancing text

EMPHASIS
Change the weight of text or use large capitals to add emphasis.

Darker lines suggest heavier weight for titles or focal point of text. There are so many possibilities.

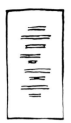
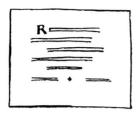

(A) THUMBNAIL SKETCHES
To decide layout and format.

Rebus in adversis
R R R

(B) RULE UP AND WRITE OUT TEXT
*Including title, etc. draw out
decoration and any large capitals.*

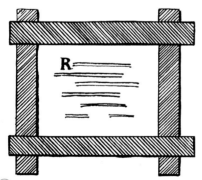

(C) CUT OUT AND PASTE DOWN
*All elements following thumbnail. Check line spacing by
matching pencil lines on cut strips to those on base paper.*

(D) FIND BEST TEXT-TO-SPACE RATIO
Use dark card strips.

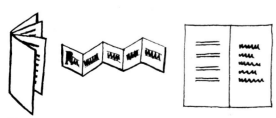

(E) COLOUR TRIALS AND MOCK UP
(if appropriate)

MAKE A PASTE-UP LAYOUT: With your chosen design in mind (A), rule up and write out the text in ink using the sizes, weights and colours you think will suit the shape of the finished work. Write or draw out any extra decoration or large capitals (B). Cut out all the elements into strips or individual pieces. Assemble all the pieces on a sheet of plain paper, following the thumbnail sketch (C). You may want to make changes – a layout at full size can often have quite a different feel when compared to the initial sketch. Rewrite incorporating any changes and continue to assemble the pieces in this way until you are satisfied with the result. Use strips of dark coloured card to decide the margins around the lettering (D).

Draw out the final shape you have chosen with the aid of the card strips onto a sheet of layout paper. Use a paper ruler to transfer the appropriate line spacing and rule up, as described on page 22. Stick everything into place using a repositionable glue; it allows you to move the pieces about easily to get the text accurately squared up with the lines on the layout paper.

Lay some tracing paper over your paste-up to disguise the patch marks of the stuck-down pieces and give a better idea of the finished effect. Check the margins again with the card strips, adjusting them if necessary.

Before you start the finished work, if you are going to use a coloured paper, remember that it will look rather different compared to plain black on white, so it is worth taking the time to do a trial paste-up with the materials you intend to use (E). Make a mock-up for books.

Measure and cut your chosen final paper to size (plus an allowance for trimming out). Tack it down onto the drawing board with masking tape and rule it up using the paste-up and paper ruler as your guide, then write out the text with confidence (F).

Rebus

(F) RULE UP AND WRITE OUT FINISHED PIECE

developing
projects

The projects that follow will ease you through the stages of planning and executing a complete design, reminding you of the different processes and making most of the design decisions for you, but you might like to make alternative choices to adapt the ideas and make them your own.

letterhead with monogram

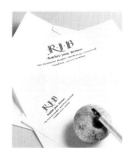

This project designs some simple, personalized stationery using a monogram of decorated letters. It combines three elements into a balanced design, using three nib sizes, and shows how to make artwork for conventional printing in two colours.

specific materials

Essential equipment (see pages 8–9)

Dip pen and nibs, Nos $2\frac{1}{2}$, $3\frac{1}{2}$ and 4

Gouache, scarlet lake and opaque white

Brushes and palette for mixing gouache

Repositionable glue

Thin white card, 200 gsm minimum

T-square

Set square

A4 (297 x 210 mm/$11\frac{1}{2}$ x $8\frac{1}{4}$ in) white wove paper, 100 gsm (such as Conqueror), this could be ordered from the printer

1 Look again at the design practicalities discussed on page 36. With these concepts in mind, think about the design of the piece. Remember that the size and position of the monogram and address should not be too big, allowing enough room for the writing beneath. The positioning of the design should look right when the paper is folded to go in the envelope. Will the correspondence on this letterhead be hand-written or typed? This may have a bearing on the style and position of the design on the page.

2 Start by drafting out ideas as thumbnail sketches including the three elements of monogram, name and address, working towards a balanced layout.

3 Work on the monogram, starting with pencil scribbles then moving onto pen roughs (1). I have picked a hollow versal written with a slanted pen, using a No. $2\frac{1}{2}$ nib for the letters and a No. 4 nib for the bud decoration. Try out different colours for the letters.

4 Choose an appropriate script for the name and address (2). I have used a plain italic which complements the style of the monogram, but does not detract from it. Rule up and write out the wording, balancing the size of these two elements against the monogram. I settled on a No. $3\frac{1}{2}$ nib for the name and a No. 4 nib for the rest.

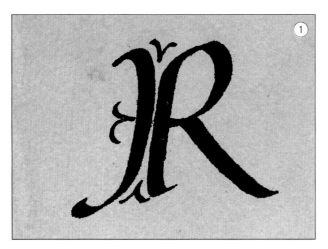

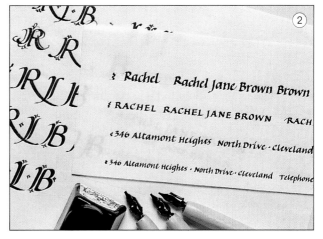

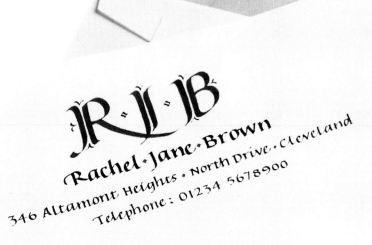

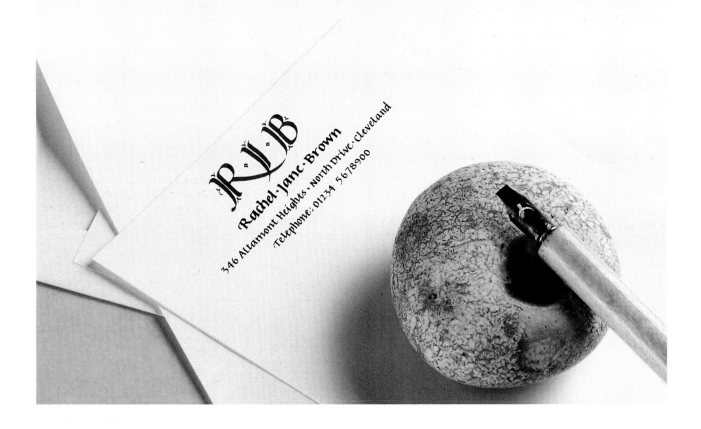

5 Mark the centres of each line, then cut out the lettering (or photocopies of it) and make an A4 paste-up layout, assessing the correct line spacing as you put all the elements in place (3).

6 Finalize the lettering at the x-height on the paste-up by practising until you are confident to go ahead with the finished version. Sort out any problems with spacing and colour (4).

7 Write everything out again, neatly, on a fresh sheet of layout paper. Repeat the monogram in black ink only, tidying up any rough edges with opaque white gouache.

8 Now to make the artwork for printing. First make a paper ruler, marking up the x-heights and baselines from your paste-up. Rule up an A4-sized rectangle onto thin card. Using a T-square and set square, transfer the measurements from the paper ruler to the card and rule them in lightly.

9 Trim out all the elements of the neatly rewritten version. Put them face down on some clean scrap paper and spread a thin layer of glue on the back, one piece at a time. Position each piece accurately on the card, matching the pencil centre and baselines. Clean off any surplus glue carefully with a plastic eraser or a ball of dried cow gum, and erase all pencil lines. Add trim marks at the corners of what will be an A4 sheet.

10 Cover the card with tracing paper. On this overlay mark up instructions for the printer, specifying colours and type of paper (5). You can use coloured pencils or felt-tip pens (to approximate the colour you have specified in your instructions) to colour in the letters so that the printer knows your intention exactly.

11 If you wish, you can reduce the complete design by about 50% on a photocopier and make another piece of artwork, as previously described, for A6 headed notecards (148 x 105 mm/$5\frac{3}{4}$ x $4\frac{1}{8}$ in) or with the monogram only, for matching envelopes.

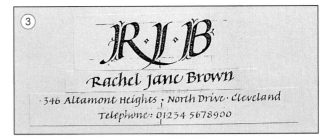

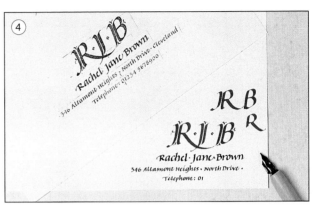

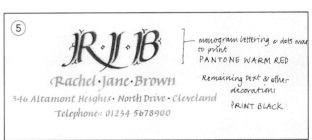

alternatives

The monogram can be as simple or as complex as you wish to make it. Here are some ideas, based on versals, which could be used as a basis for your design. These letters would work in one or two colours and could be used in many other ways, for example as initial letters at the start of a piece of poetry or prose.

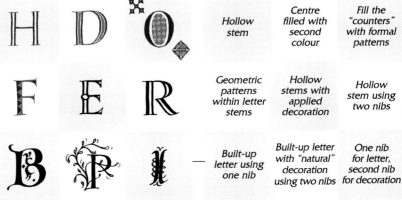

Hollow stem	*Centre filled with second colour* · *Fill the "counters" with formal patterns*
Geometric patterns within letter stems	*Hollow stems with applied decoration* · *Hollow stem using two nibs*
Built-up letter using one nib	*Built-up letter with "natural" decoration using two nibs* · *One nib for letter, second nib for decoration*

greetings card

I have made cards like this for family and friends for as long as I can remember, and still enjoy the challenge of coming up with fresh ideas. Your design need not be complex to be effective; you could pick a series of phrases like these, all connected with birthday, celebrations and good wishes, and then use your design skills to dovetail them together. This project uses two styles and three weights of lettering; modern versals with calligraphic weighting, italic capitals and a cursive italic. It employs change of weight, colour and direction of writing for its impact and interest.

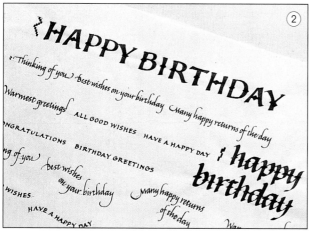

specific materials

Essential equipment (see pages 8–9)

Dip pen and nibs, Nos $2\frac{1}{2}$, and 4

Repositionable glue

Gouache, scarlet lake, cadmium yellow and gold

Brushes and palette for mixing gouache

1 sheet HP watercolour paper, 300 gsm

Sable brushes, Nos 0 and 00

Scalpel, cutting mat and metal ruler

Bone folder

1 sheet coloured paper, approximately 150 gsm

9H pencil for transferring design

finished size

92 x 205 mm ($3\frac{5}{8}$ x 8 in) when folded

1 Make thumbnail sketches to experiment with a design, trying both landscape and portrait formats (1).

2 Write out your chosen text on layout paper. Here, the versals are written at ten nib-widths of a No. $2\frac{1}{2}$ nib to give bold, chunky letters as the centrepiece; the lightly spiky cursive italics with flourished extensions have an x-height of four nib-widths of a No. 4 nib and the italic capitals are at the same height. Write the phrases on straight lines first, before drawing out gently curving lines and writing out the text again (2). This will need some practice to get right, as the uprights should follow the tilt of the curve. Experiment with the flourishes as well.

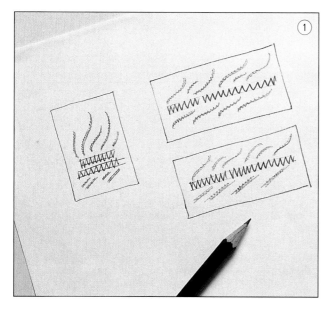

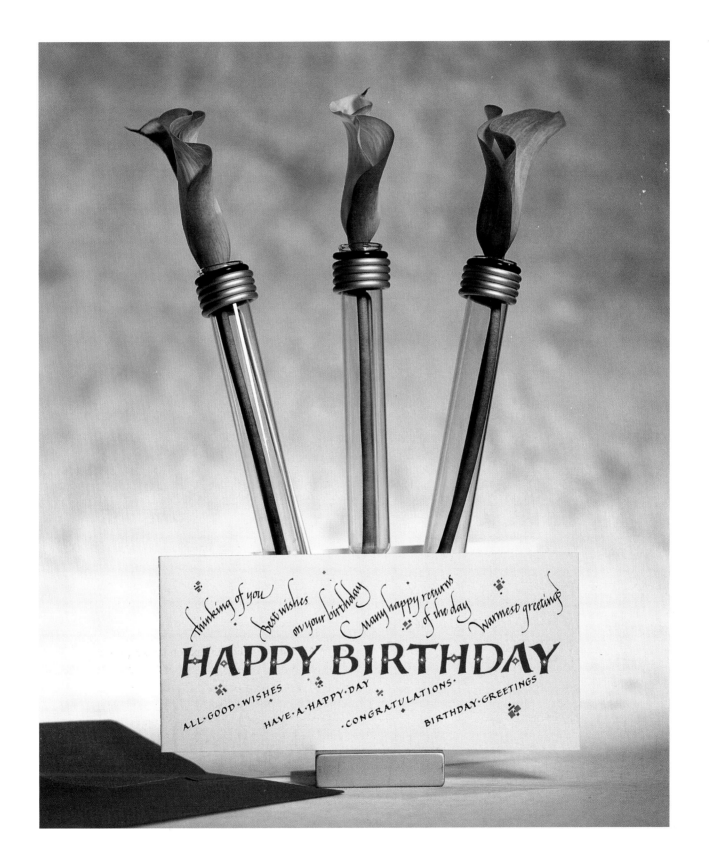

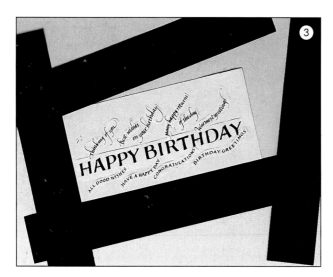

3 Cut out these elements (or photocopies of them) to make paste-ups. I made two to help decide on the design, using strips of black card to indicate the margins (3 and 4). I decided to alter the capitals on curves back to straight lines to avoid a fussy design. It is easier to see and make decisions about this sort of problem at full size.

4 Make another paste-up with an overlay roughed in to show colour and decoration on the main wording (5).

5 On a sheet of tracing paper, trace off the chunky versals and the position of the lines for the rest of the text, marking them accurately. If you are not confident about writing on curves straight onto the card, trace in this wording carefully as well (6).

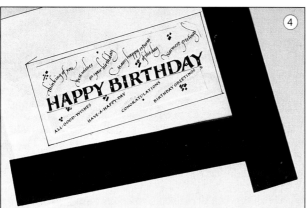

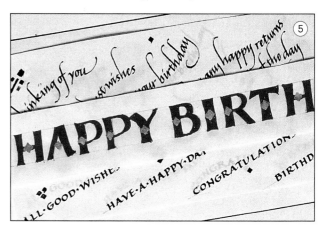

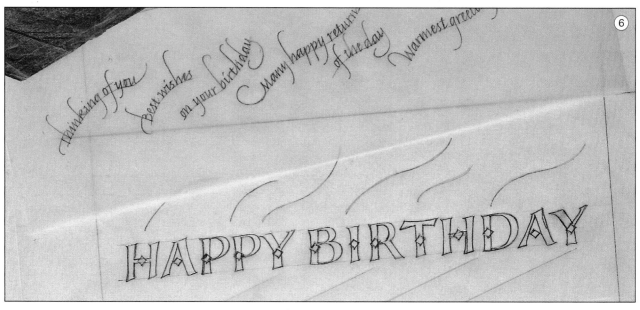

6 Tack the watercolour paper to the drawing board and rule up the full dimensions of the card (remember to double the width measurement and mark the fold) with trim all round. Transfer your design to the paper (see page 36).

7 Before you do any writing on the finished piece, try ink and paint out first on a spare scrap of the watercolour paper, as you may need to give the surface a dusting of pounce for the writing to be crisp.

8 Complete the cursive italics and the italic caps in black ink first (7). Then mix some scarlet lake gouache with a touch of cadmium yellow and begin outlining the versals, using a No. 00 sable brush. Fill in the letters carefully, using a No. 0 sable brush, leaving the diamonds in the letters blank (8).

9 Fill in the decorative diamonds in the large red letters using gold gouache. To give an extra sparkle and to help balance the design, devise little groups of red, gold and black diamonds on layout paper, which can be moved about on the rough until you are satisfied with their position. Transfer these patterns to the finished piece with pen or brush.

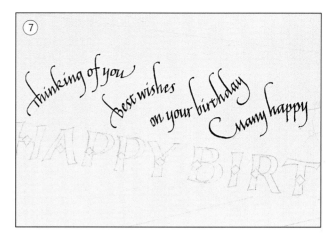

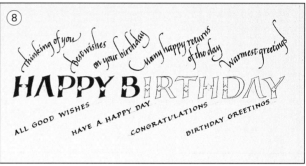

10 Trim out the finished card using a scalpel against a metal ruler. Use a bone folder to make a clean, sharp fold in the card.

11 To complete the project, you might like to make your own envelope, especially if the card is not a standard size. The following template and formula can be adapted to any shape.

Make the template on layout paper by drawing a rectangle 8 mm ($\frac{5}{8}$ in) longer and wider than the finished greetings card. B = $\frac{3}{4}$ of A; C = $\frac{1}{2}$ of A; D and E = 25 mm (1 in) minimum, wider for a bigger envelope. Angle the top part of D and E and round the corners off to make it easier to slip the card into the envelope.

Transfer the template to coloured paper, then cut the envelope out with a scalpel against a metal ruler, using scissors for the round corners. Score along the dotted lines by aligning the ruler against the pencil line and pressing down with the pointed end of a bone folder. Press all folds flat (B over D and E) and apply glue. Take care not to use too much – slip scrap paper under the flaps to catch any excess.

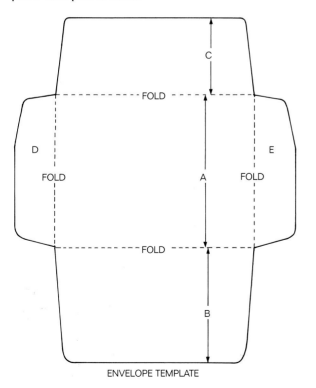

ENVELOPE TEMPLATE

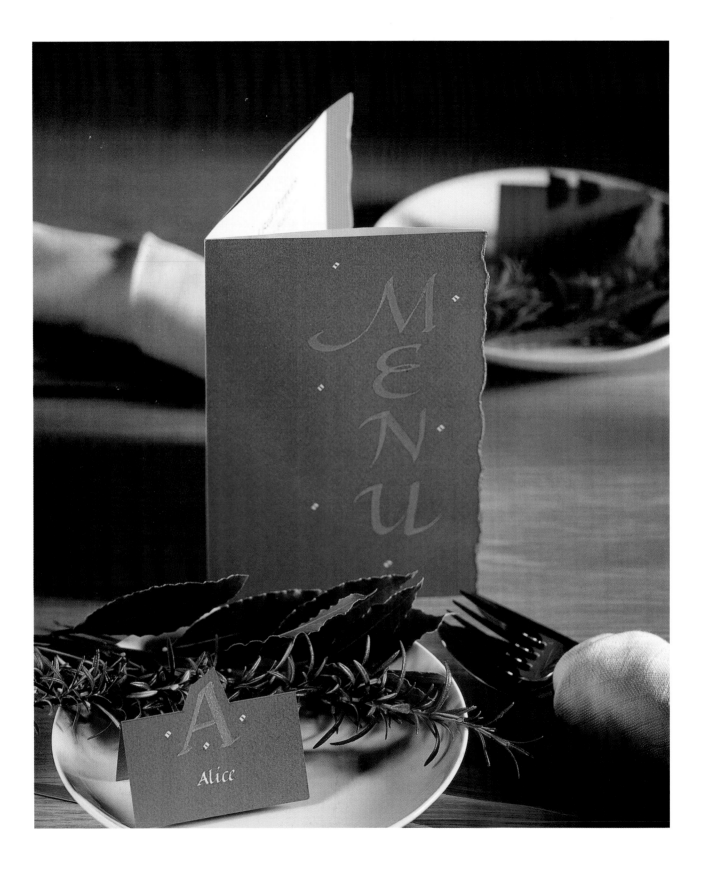

menu and matching
place cards

To design a menu and matching place cards you will need to think carefully about the concepts discussed on page 36. You will also need to decide the number of dishes and courses to be served. In this case, the menu is for an informal, three-course summer dinner party at home, for which you need only make one or two menus by hand. For a larger, more formal occasion, you could consider designing something more classic and preparing artwork to have printed (see page 43). I have chosen to use a mid-toned paper for the cover, with a marble-patterned inner sheet – the fresh greens reflect an early summer feel.

specific materials

Cover paper: 1 sheet Canson mi-teintes, 160 gsm,
   No. 575 (green)
Menu paper: 1 sheet G F Smith Marlmarque, 90 gsm,
   Corinthian green
Dip pen and nibs, Nos $3\frac{1}{2}$ and 4
Automatic pen, No. 3
Repositionable glue
Gouache, mistletoe green, cadmium yellow, gold
   and opaque white
Brushes and palette for mixing gouache
Gum sandarach (optional)
White pencil (for transferring design)
Scalpel, cutting mat and metal ruler
Bone folder

finished size of menu

folded from A4 (297 x 210 mm/$11\frac{1}{2}$ x $8\frac{1}{4}$ in),
front flap 137 mm ($5\frac{3}{8}$ in) wide

1 Decide on the approximate size of the menu card and inner pages. I used an A4 sheet folded asymmetrically for the cover. The inner pages need to be approximately 4 mm ($\frac{1}{8}$ in) narrower over all than the cover, to allow for the fold and the deckle edges. Jot down your ideas for cover and inner pages in thumbnail sketches. Think about the most appropriate style of writing for both parts, the type of decoration you might like to incorporate and how the design could be adapted to suit the place cards.

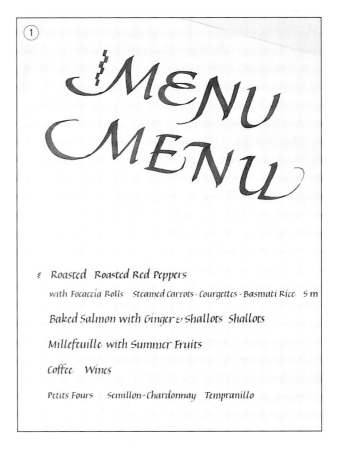

2 Rule up layout paper and write out all the wording for the menu in your chosen hand, deciding the appropriate weights and sizes for the page size and amount of text (1).

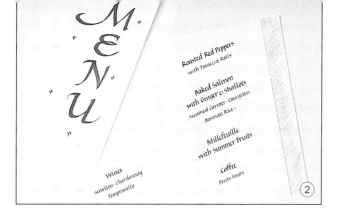

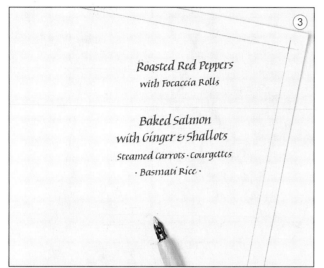

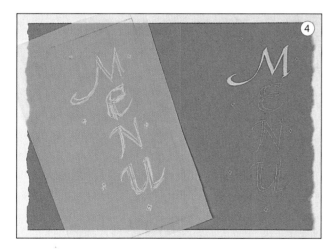

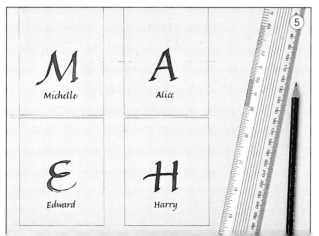

3 Draft some flourished italic capitals for the cover using the automatic pen, and make paste-ups for both cover and menu pages, with careful consideration of the position of the text on the page (2). It is important to standardize on a consistent line space throughout to achieve unity in the design.

4 Mix up some of the paint colours you are going to use (mistletoe green and cadmium yellow to match the cover paper, gold for flourished capitals and white for decorations) and try them out, as well as the black ink, on the papers for each section and decide how you will use the colour to best effect. You may need a dusting of gum sandarach on the paper to make the writing crisp.

5 When you are happy with the spacing on the paste-up, measure out and rule up the paper for the cover and menu pages following this layout carefully, leaving a trim allowance all round. Write out the menu text first and leave to dry (3).

6 Do a trace of the lettering for the cover and transfer to the green paper (see page 37) using a white pencil – instead of a carbon pencil which will not show up on this mid-toned paper. Make sure you have enough gold gouache mixed up, then write in the flourished capitals that you have traced down, using the automatic pen. Add the white decorations when the gold is dry (4).

7 To complete the menu, trim out the inner pages with a scalpel and metal ruler, score and fold using a bone folder (see page 8). Trim the top and bottom edges only of the cover, score and fold, then make deckle edges as described opposite, painting the torn edges with gold gouache as a finishing touch.

8 Run a strip of glue down the inner edge of the inside back cover and attach the menu pages, pressing down firmly.

9 To make place cards, work out a suitable size (see diagram, opposite), to accommodate initials and names at the same sizes used for the menu. Rule up and write the initials and names on layout paper (5).

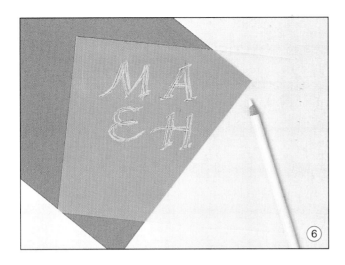

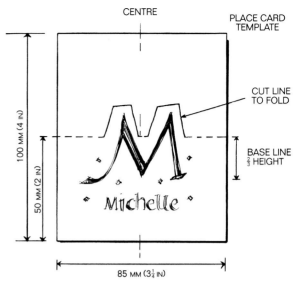

CENTRE

CUT LINE
TO FOLD

100 MM (4 IN)

50 MM (2 IN)

BASE LINE
⅔ HEIGHT

Michelle

85 MM (3¼ IN)

Mark the centres, cut out the elements and make a paste-up for all the cards. The capitals sit on a baseline ⅔ of the capital height below the fold.

10 Draw out rectangles for all the place cards on the green card, rule up and transfer the initials as before (6), then do the writing in gold and white gouache (7). Pencil in trim marks around the top of the initials and cut out with a scalpel. Trim out the rest of the card, turn each one over, pencil in the halfway mark, score up to the cut edges round the capital and fold carefully right way up, making sure the top edge of the letter stands up clearly.

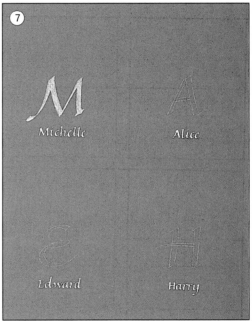

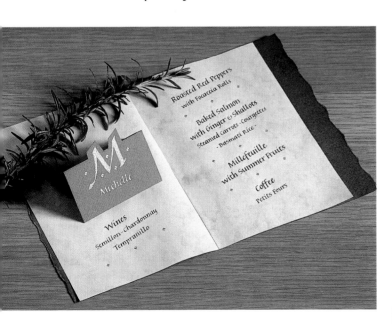

To make a "straight" edge, instead of ruling a pencil line where the deckle edge is required, score a straight line with a bone folder. For a "wavy" edge, score the line in freehand with a bone folder or the back of a scalpel blade, pressing down firmly. This helps to crush the fibres in preparation for the next stage.

Using an eye dropper or a paintbrush, trail distilled water along the crease you have made and leave it to soak in and soften the fibres for about 10 minutes (thicker papers will take longer). With the paper flat, using an even amount of pull on each side, slowly ease the crease apart sideways then leave to dry. It will dry slightly rough and cockled, rather like a true deckled edge.

making deckle edges

combining text
and translation

This project, combining a Latin proverb with a translation in English in a single opening manuscript book, is a logical progression from the earlier exercises working with alphabets of different styles and weights. You could choose your own pieces in whatever languages, the principles outlined below remain the same. Here I have chosen a fairly traditional colour scheme, but reversed the normal pattern and written in white on black paper, which looks quite dramatic.

specific materials
Essential equipment (see pages 8–9)
Dip pen and nibs, Nos 3 and 4
Repositionable glue
Gouache, scarlet lake, Venetian red and opaque white
Brushes and palette for mixing gouache
Text pages: 1 sheet Canson mi-teintes, 160 gsm, No. 425 (black)
Cover paper: 1 sheet Canson mi-teintes, 160 gsm, No. 130 (terracotta)
Interleaf: 1 sheet Thai tissue (peach)
Scalpel, cutting mat and metal ruler
Bone folder
Black embroidery thread and needle

finished size of book
open cover 205 x 220 mm (8 x $8\frac{5}{8}$ in)
open tissue interleaf 195 x 190 mm ($7\frac{5}{8}$ x $7\frac{1}{2}$ in)
open text pages 190 x 176 mm ($7\frac{1}{2}$ x 7 in)
folds to 205 x 88 mm (8 x $3\frac{1}{2}$ in)

1 When you have chosen your original text and its translation, you will need to decide which of the two is to form the main focus of the piece. Here are some guidelines to help you put a design together.

☐ There should be no visual conflict between the two texts, so the eye follows each language easily, without any confusion.
☐ Try to link phrase with phrase to retain the sense of the words in both languages.
☐ If the authors' names are known, include these in the design, they may help the balance of the piece.
☐ Choose the calligraphic style carefully to suit the text.

2 To achieve importance of one text over the other, try one or more of the following suggestions:

☐ Two different letter styles.
☐ Two different nib sizes, the same letter style (the two texts will often differ in length, a smaller nib for the longer version will shorten the lines).
☐ Capitals for the main text, lower case for the translation (or vice versa).
☐ Use two colours or two tones of one colour.

3 Layout possibilities are many and varied, although the length and content of your texts and the intended final form of the piece (broadsheet, manuscript book, for example) will be the deciding factors. Start by making thumbnail sketches to plan your ideas, then rule up layout paper and write out both texts in the hand and size you feel will suit the design (1).

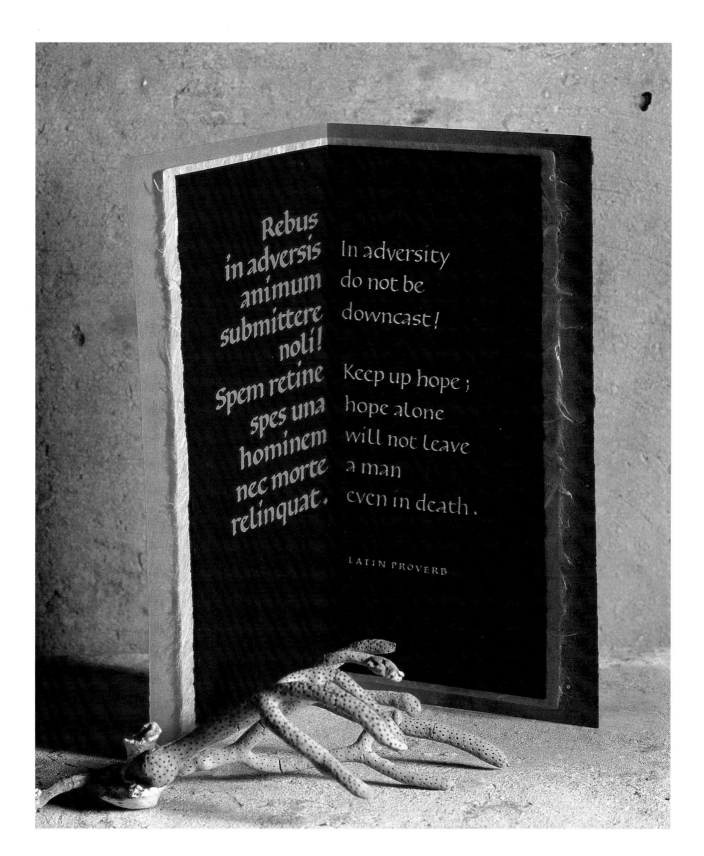

Rebus
in adversis
animum
submittere
noli!
Spem retine
spes una
hominem
nec morte
relinquat.

In adversity
do not be
downcast!

Keep up hope ;
hope alone
will not leave
a man
even in death.

LATIN PROVERB

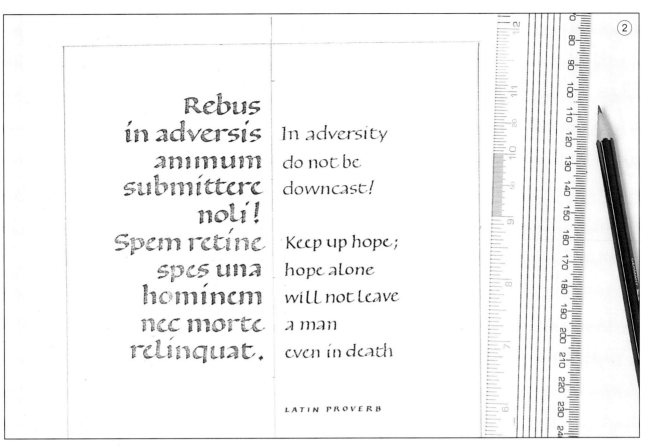

Rebus
in adversis
animum
submittere
noli!
Spem retine
spes una
hominem
nec morte
relinquat.

In adversity
do not be
downcast!

Keep up hope;
hope alone
will not leave
a man
even in death

LATIN PROVERB

4 Adjust the size to weight ratio if necessary. I have used a No. 3 nib at three nib-widths x-height, foundation hand, for the Latin, to give solid weight. The translation is written in the same hand with a No. 4 nib at normal x-height of four nib-widths (the capital height is actually the same as the x-height of the Latin, which gives a sense of unity to the piece).

5 Cut out the strips of lettering (or photocopies) and try out the various permutations before making a paste-up layout. Here, I found that the line breaks worked best in a portrait rather than landscape format, keeping the sense in both languages (2). The line spacing is kept the same for both pages to help with unity; the extra line space before the attribution on the right-hand page helps balance the design. The margins of the final paste-up are based on the classic "golden section" formula: the top and outer margins are twice the gutter (margin down the centre of the page); the bottom margin is twice the outer margin (see diagram).

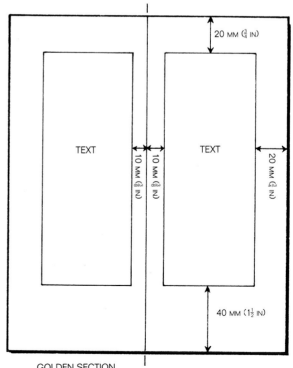

20 MM (¾ IN)

TEXT

TEXT

10 MM (⅜ IN)

10 MM (⅜ IN)

20 MM (¾ IN)

40 MM (1½ IN)

GOLDEN SECTION

6 Before you start the finished piece, mix up some gouache (scarlet lake, Venetian red and a little white to match the terracotta cover) and try it out to make sure it is opaque enough to be read easily on the black paper (3). The writing is done on the smooth reverse side of the paper.

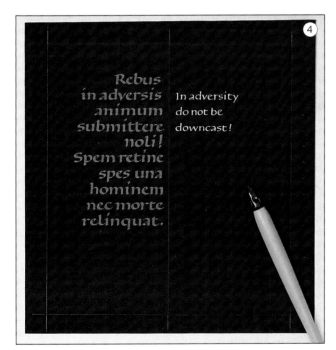

7 Measure out (leaving trim allowance all round) and transfer line positions onto the outer edge of the black paper. Rule up lightly so the lines are just visible, accurately following the line lengths on the final layout. This saves having to erase excess lines, which may mark the paper. Remember your pages must fold along the paper grain, not against it. Write the left-hand page first and leave to dry, then the right (4).

8 Measure and cut out both the cover paper and the tissue interleaf – use a scalpel and metal ruler for the top and bottom edges, but give the leading (outer) edges a deckled finish (see page 51) (5). Trim out the black text pages in the same way.

9 To assemble the book, score and fold the three sections (cover, pages and interleaf) with a bone folder. The cover should have the textured surface on the outside. Mark the black pages with the position of the sewing holes along the fold (see diagram, below). Gather the pages together, hold them firmly in position on a flat surface to maintain the even margins all round (you could tack them down lightly with masking tape) and prick the holes with a needle through all three layers (5). Sew the book following the diagram, finishing with a neatly tied reef knot in the centre. Snip off excess thread with scissors.

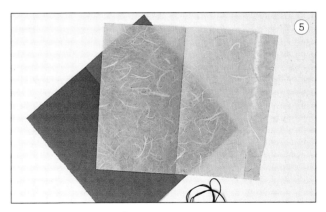

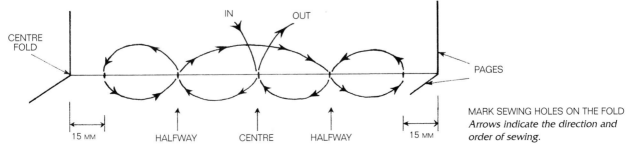

MARK SEWING HOLES ON THE FOLD
Arrows indicate the direction and order of sewing.

multilingual calendar

This multilingual calendar is a complex project to put together, but offers plenty of scope for creative calligraphic ideas. It involves experimentation with size and weight of drawn and painted letterforms, the use of both coloured and textured papers, as well as sorting out some tricky design problems.

I wanted to produce a finished piece that had an appropriate seasonal feel, with numbers easily visible when the calendar was hung up. I decided to break the year down into the four seasons and chose appropriately coloured and interestingly textured papers to reflect this scheme. I wanted the calligraphic designs to be based on pen-written, or drawn and painted letters with minimal or no decoration, which would in some way symbolize the month and season.

papers

Season	Base papers (handmade) ~ Month overlays
Winter	Khadi neutral ~ Canson mi-teintes, 160 gsm, blue
Spring	Khadi algae (green threads) ~ Ingres, 160 gsm, yellow-green
Summer	Khadi marigold (yellow petals) ~ Canson mi-teintes, 160 gsm, orange
Autumn	Khadi straw (dried grass stems) ~ Ingres, 160 gsm, rusty-brown

other materials

Essential equipment (see pages 8–9)
Dip pen and nibs, Nos $1\frac{1}{2}$ and 5
Repositionable glue
Coloured pencils, basic range
Gouache, from basic range, colours to tone with
    month overlay paper
Brushes and palette for mixing gouache
2 sheets each of Khadi papers (see left), allows for
    colour trials and possible errors
1 sheet each of coloured papers (see left), allows for
    colour trials and possible errors
Double hole puncher
Neutral embroidery thread
Piece of bamboo cane

finished size of calendar

227 x 385 mm ($8\frac{3}{4}$ x $15\frac{1}{8}$ in)
with month overlays 227 x 122 mm ($8\frac{3}{4}$ x $5\frac{3}{4}$ in)

1 Start by making thumbnail sketches of the basic design of the base pages. Use the size of the base paper and how it can be divided economically to help you decide on proportion and format. The Khadi papers will cut into four good-sized pieces; three for finished pages and one spare for practice. These papers are handmade and have wonderful deckle edges, so, rather than lose the character of the material when you cut the pages out for ruling up, use the deckle method (see page 51).

2 Write out the days on layout paper in five languages and the dates at the letter heights you think will suit. The numbers need to be fairly bold for ease of legibility

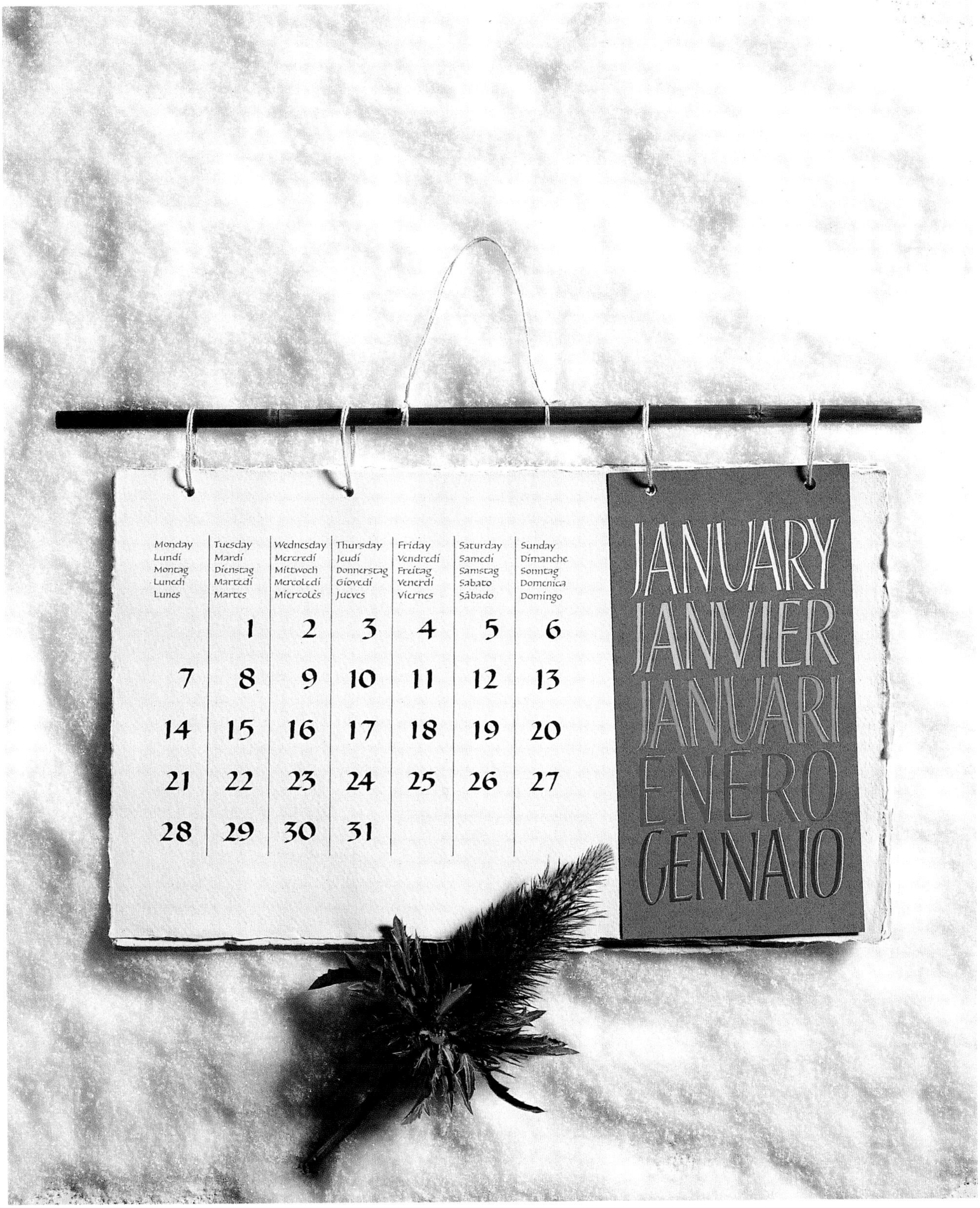

Monday	Tuesday	Wednesday	Thursday	Friday	Saturday	Sunday
Lundi	Mardi	Mercredi	Jeudi	Vendredi	Samedi	Dimanche
Montag	Dienstag	Mittwoch	Donnerstag	Freitag	Samstag	Sonntag
Lunedì	Martedì	Mercoledì	Giovedì	Venerdì	Sabato	Domenica
Lunes	Martes	Miercolès	Jueves	Viernes	Sàbado	Domingo
	1	2	3	4	5	6
7	8	9	10	11	12	13
14	15	16	17	18	19	20
21	22	23	24	25	26	27
28	29	30	31			

JANUARY
JANVIER
JANUARI
ENERO
GENNAIO

(written with a No. 1½ nib), the days smaller and lighter in weight so that they will fit into fairly narrow columns (written with a No. 5 nib).

3 Cut all the elements or photocopies into strips. Draw up a rectangle on layout paper corresponding to the final paper size. Work out and draw in the column widths, then make a paste-up of the whole page. You may need to alter letter and/or number sizes to fit. Consider the use of a second colour to enhance the design.

4 Work up some ideas for the month overlays from small sketches to same-size layouts – I like to do these on tracing paper, laying one on top of the other, refining the lettering at each stage. Start to get some idea of how you will use colour on these overlays. Photocopy the trace layouts onto plain paper and fill them in with coloured pencils to help you experiment. Here are some of the styles of lettering and colouring that I used:

❑ January (1): Long thin letters look like icicles or snow on snow. Graduated shades of blue are used with monoline white "shadows".
❑ April (2): Strands of spiky letters wave upwards like growing plants, in spring yellows and greens. Flecks of red give a touch of vibrancy.
❑ August (3): Hot summer shades of red move out to white on a bright background, like a blazing sun. Dots of the complementary colour, cobalt, are added as punctuation.
❑ October (2): Mellow shades of autumn are used and the letters are piled up like fallen leaves.

The designs for the months in between could carry on the "flavour" set by these ideas. Decoration, if any, is restricted to tiny flashes of complementary colours.

5 All the lettering should be drawn, then painted. Do paint and ink trials on spare pieces of all the papers before you begin the preparations for the finished work. Use the smooth side of the coloured papers (4).

6 The simplest way to mark up all the base pages uniformly is to make a paper template on which you indicate the position of everything. Transfer these marks lightly onto each sheet and rule up ready to write. To avoid too much bulk on one side of the calendar, the position of the month overlays alternates from the right- to the left-hand side, so make allowance for this on the template.

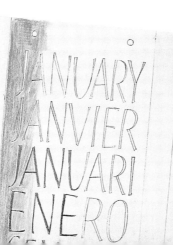

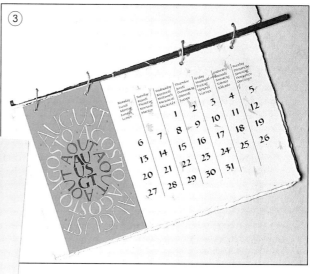

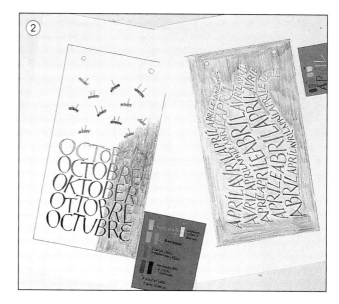

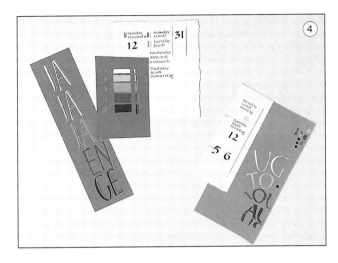

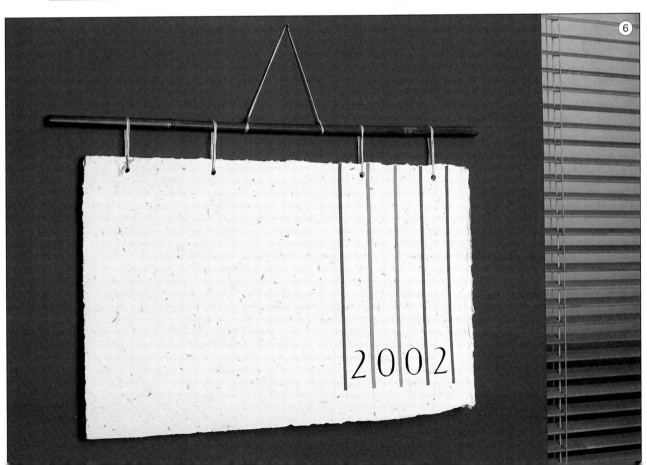

7 Write the days and put in the dividing rules in the colour for each month first, then the numbers in black ink (5). Organize the work to suit yourself; you may prefer to do one base and overlay at a time and see some progress, rather than spending ages just on ruling up.

8 When you have completed all the bases and overlays, think about a design for the cover and sketch out some ideas. My solution was to cut out strips of the four coloured papers and stick them onto a sheet of the neutral Khadi paper with large black numerals between (6).

9 The binding should be simple and practical so that pages can be turned easily. Devise a method of marking the pages, so you know where to position the punch correctly each time and do trials on scrap paper. One pair of holes should be centred over the overlays at each side. Punch the pages, then put together with loops of embroidery thread, tied with reef knots. Cut a length of slim bamboo cane slightly wider than the calendar pages, slip this through the thread loops and add a separate thread for hanging, knotting it tightly onto the cane midway between the pairs of holes.

pushing out
the boundaries

Most of the techniques and projects you have tackled so far have been fairly conservative in their treatment of letterforms, enabling you to learn the principles of calligraphy and understand them first. Now, with that knowledge under your belt, is the time to push out the boundaries and explore some exciting new possibilities. Try using unusual tools to write with, see how much you can stretch or compress letterforms before legibility is lost, find out about new techniques to extend your repertoire. Have fun!

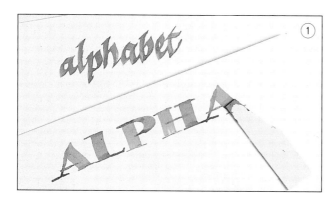

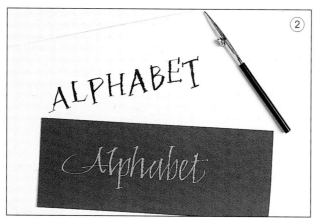

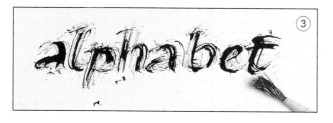

new tools

The following tools, both commercial and homemade, can be used with paints and inks to create exciting new effects.

CARD PENS: Cut some 1 mm ($\frac{1}{32}$ in) thick card into strips of different widths and dip these into coloured inks to use as you would a normal dip pen (1). Hold the "nib" end at the appropriate angle and try copying the exemplars (see pages 24–31). You can make very big pens in this way, and strips of wood veneer or chunks of thick felt held in a bulldog clip are effective alternatives. You will need to pour out your ink or mix paint in palettes or saucers that are large enough to accommodate these big pens.

RULING PENS: These are usually used to draw fine, even lines, but they also make effective writing tools (2). The narrower type need to be held on their side to make broad lines. Try pearly or metallic inks on dark paper or bright acrylics on rough watercolour paper. Don't worry about the splatters you make, they can be incorporated into the design.

ROUGH STRING: Rough, garden twine can be a little unpredictable for writing or drawing with, but it can also produce some very interesting and decorative effects that can be exploited for modern designs (3). Bind a piece of string around the middle with masking tape. Dip into paint or ink and use it as you would a normal pen.

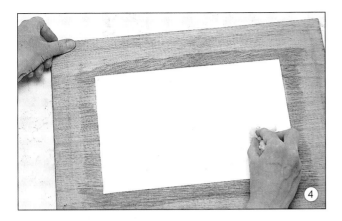

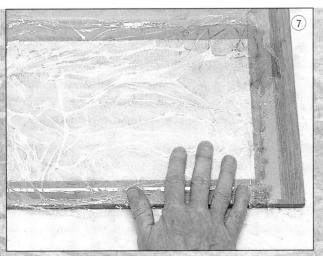

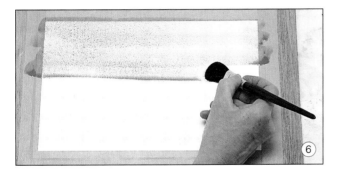

new backgrounds

There are a number of simple techniques you can employ to make interesting backgrounds for your calligraphy projects.

STRETCHING THE PAPER: Before you can lay a painted watercolour background, the paper has to be stretched to prevent it cockling as it dries. Immerse the paper in a tray of cold water, or hold it under running water, making sure both sides are evenly wet. Drain off excess water and lay the sheet carefully onto a clean, plywood drawing board which is larger than the paper. Blot the surface with a dry sponge, but do not "scrub" at the paper or the surface will be spoilt (4).

Cut four strips of gummed paper tape (one for each side of the paper). Damp one strip at a time with a wet sponge and use it to stick the damp watercolour paper to the board, allowing a 10 mm ($\frac{3}{8}$ in) overlap onto the paper. When all the sides have been taped down, lay the board flat and allow to dry out completely (5).

TEXTURED BACKGROUND: To make a textured background, stretch the paper as described above and leave it on the board. Lay a wash of watercolour paint, well diluted, over the paper with a wide, soft brush (6). While the paint is still wet, lay a piece of transparent food wrap (cling film) over it, and pull the food wrap together slightly (7). Leave it to dry flat. Remove the food wrap to reveal a rather interesting, batik-type finish, over which you can write with gouache or ink.

PASTEL BACKGROUND: To make a soft and subtle background "wash", scrape a pastel stick with a knife onto a smooth or slightly textured paper (8). Rub the resulting powder into the surface with cotton wool (9). Experiment with blending colours. You may need to seal the pastel with a light spray of fixative before writing over it either with gouache or ink.

OIL PASTEL BACKGROUND: Scribble with an oil pastel onto a piece of cartridge or smooth watercolour paper to create a thick, even layer, blending the colours (if more than one is used) with your fingers (10). Letters or designs can be scratched into the oil pastel using the point of a scalpel blade or an old broad-edged nib (11).

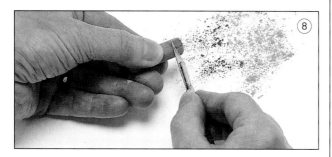

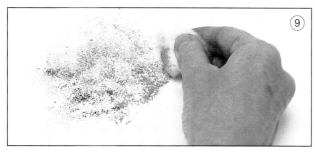

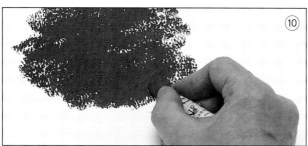

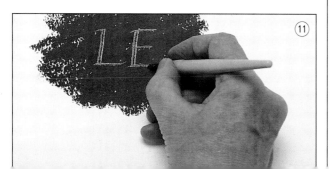

resists

Masking fluid is used in watercolour painting as a resist to block out the paint. In calligraphy we can use it to write or draw a motif that will not absorb a subsequent wash or paint. Gouache resist works in a similar way, but the writing is done with white gouache and waterproof inks are used for the colour overlays.

MASKING FLUID: You can write with masking fluid using broad-edged nibs, as well as with a brush: use an old, or synthetic brush for this. Both nib and brush will need a good wash out with warm, soapy water after use. Write without a reservoir on the nib, draw or paint a design with the masking fluid onto paper of a reasonable weight (12). Allow to dry (it will have a matt appearance).

Mix up some paint and apply a colourwash to the paper. You can add other toning or contrasting colours when the first wash is still wet, allowing the colours to mingle (13). Leave to dry out completely.

Gently rub off the rubber solution with your fingers, using a circular motion, to reveal white letters out of a coloured ground (14 and 15). Don't rub too hard or the paper surface will be damaged. Try experimenting with multilayers of resist and colour.

GOUACHE: Paper of about 300 gsm is best for this technique, as it will stand up well to the robust treatment and is less likely to cockle as it dries. Write or draw out a design, using white gouache (tinted with a touch of yellow ochre to make it visible on white paper) and allow to dry hard (16). Use a hairdryer to speed this up.

Brush coloured waterproof ink quickly over the design, dropping in other colours if you wish. Leave to dry completely, then immerse in a bath of tepid water (17). Soak until the gouache begins to dissolve – it should float off, but can be "assisted" with a sponge or brush (18). Leave to dry spread out on a flat surface (19).

On rough watercolour paper this technique gives interesting effects, especially if the letters are written with chisel-edged oil painting brushes. Paint laid thickly gives the best resist. The inks will penetrate through thinner paint giving a pale-toned result, which could be exploited in your design. Experiment with extra layers of resist and different combinations of colours. Make notes as you go, so that the effects can be repeated.

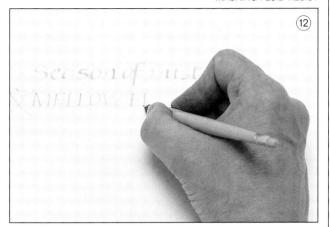

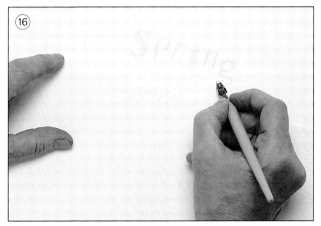

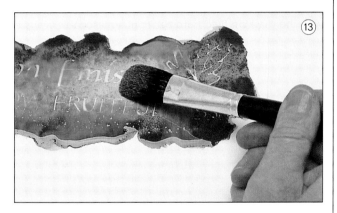

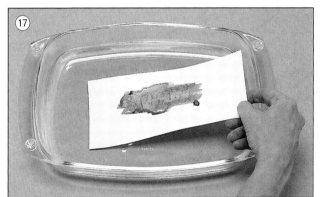

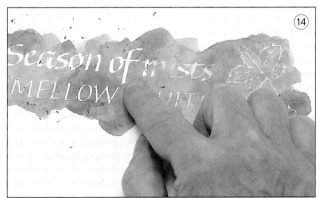

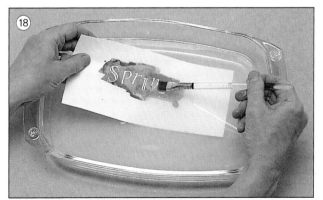

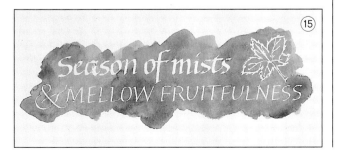

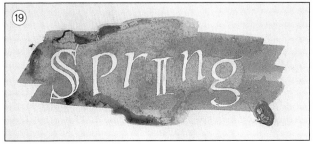

gilding

Flat gilding with transfer gold leaf is not very difficult and it will add a really luxurious shine to your work. You can gild onto most papers, although tissue paper is too thin.

For this technique you will need

Gum ammoniac solution or PVA glue mixed 50/50 with distilled water

Dip pen or synthetic brush to apply the size

Transfer gold leaf

Burnisher (or use the flat end of a bone folder – but *not* on the gold leaf)

Piece of plate glass (edges rounded)

Glassine (crystal parchment)

Soft paintbrush

Soft, clean silk

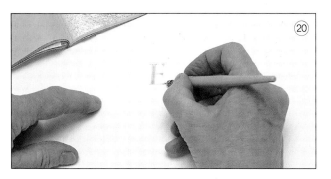

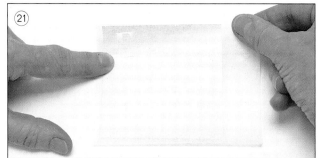

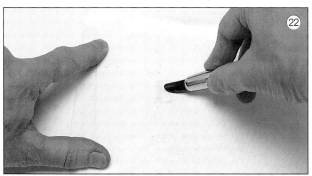

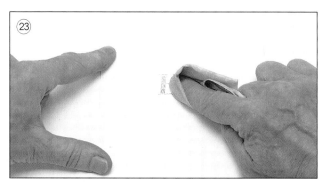

With your drawing board flat, apply the gum ammoniac or PVA solution to the paper with a dip pen (without the reservoir attached) or a brush and leave to dry for about 30 minutes (20). Breathe onto the size, three or four good, deep breaths, to make it tacky. Quickly lay a sheet of transfer gold leaf over the size and press it down firmly with your fingertips, taking care not to twist it. Rub down gently with a burnisher or bone folder, then peel back the paper to check if the gold has adhered (21). If it has not, repeat the breathing and application process until all the size is covered. You will need to apply at least two complete layers of gold.

Lay the work on a sheet of glass, with a piece of glassine over the gilded area. Gently burnish through the glassine (22). The hard surface beneath the work gives a better burnish than the drawing board. Remove the glassine and dust away surplus gold from around the edges of the letter with a soft brush. Polish with soft silk (23).

Patterns or dots can be indented into the surface of the gold leaf using a hard pencil through glassine.

christmas card

Here's another greetings card to make, this time a seasonal offering created with rough string and gold leaf.

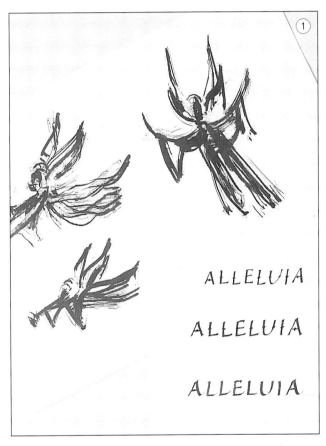

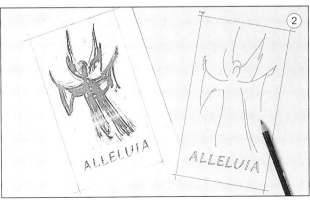

specific materials

Essential equipment (see pages 8–9)
Rough string
Dip pen and nib, No. $3\frac{1}{2}$
Repositionable glue
1 sheet of Canson mi-teintes, 160 gsm,
   No. 500 (dark blue)
PVA glue mixed 50/50 with distilled water, tinted
   with a little red gouache so it is visible on the paper
Gilding equipment (see page 64)
White pencil for transferring design
Gouache, opaque white
Brush and palette for mixing gouache
Scalpel, cutting mat and metal ruler
Bone folder

finished size of card

185 x 105 mm ($7\frac{3}{8}$ x $4\frac{1}{8}$ in) when folded

1 Do some thumbnail sketches to clarify your ideas, then start experimenting, drawing out angel shapes on layout paper at approximately finished size. Cut a length of rough string and bind it round the middle with masking tape to make it easy to hold. Dip the rough string "brush" into black ink and use it to draw the angel. This sort of technique is best reserved for fairly large-scale work requiring loose, gestural drawings. It is quite difficult to reproduce exactly the same image twice, as the string is not a precise tool. Use the dip pen to write out the wording, trying different sizes, styles and weights to find the best balance with the angel. Plain letters are best as they contrast well with the vigour of the drawing (1).

2 Make a paste-up of the image and lettering (2) – the drawing you choose will dictate whether your card is to be horizontal or vertical in format – and decide the margins using card strips. Modifications can be made at

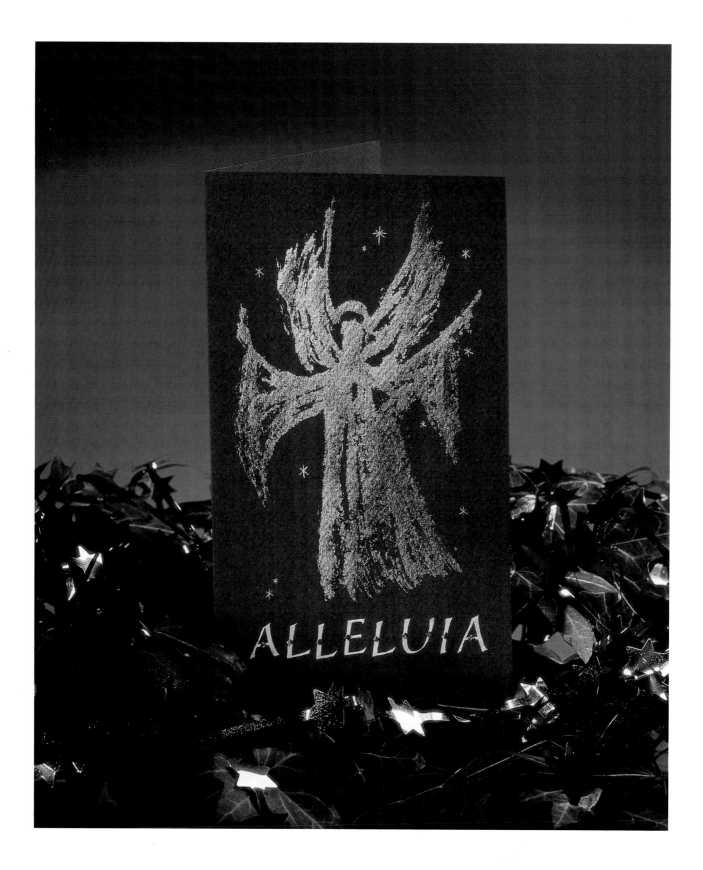

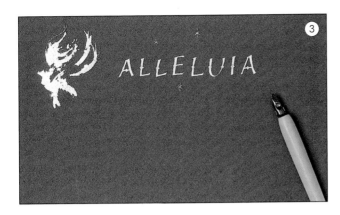

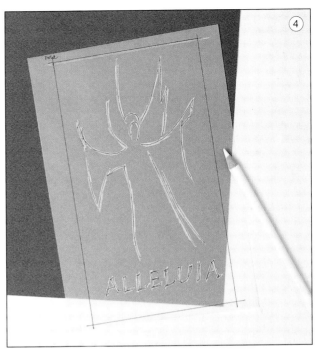

this stage. I decide to let the letters "bounce" rather than write them on a straight line, to enhance the feeling of movement, and add a few little stars to the background.

3 Try out the gilding technique (see page 64) on the blue paper, applying the size as the lettering with a dip pen without a reservoir (3). You may need to add a little more PVA to the size mixture if the gold does not stick well first time. Apply the PVA mix to the angel shape with a clean piece of string, as close as possible to your original design: put on plenty of the medium and draw out of it to make fine lines. Gild as usual.

4 Draw out the rectangle for the card (185 x 210 mm/ $7\frac{3}{8}$ x $8\frac{1}{4}$ in full size) with trim allowance all round. Trace the design and wording and transfer it to the blue paper using a white pencil (4) (see page 36).

5 Gild the angel as practised in Step 3 (5). Using opaque white gouache, write in the lettering with the dip pen. When it is dry, paint in the little diamonds on the letter stems with PVA size and gild them as before. If the gold leaf adheres to the paint, use a pointed scalpel blade to scrape it off gently and go over the letters again with a No. 000 sable brush to tidy them up if necessary.

6 Add one or two tiny white stars in the background, as on your rough design. Give the gold leaf a final polish with the soft silk, then trim out the rectangle. Mark the centre on the reverse side then score and fold with a bone folder. To remove any excess white pencil marks, use a slice of eraser cut off with a scalpel. This not only gives a sharp edge, but makes it more manoeuvrable in awkward corners.

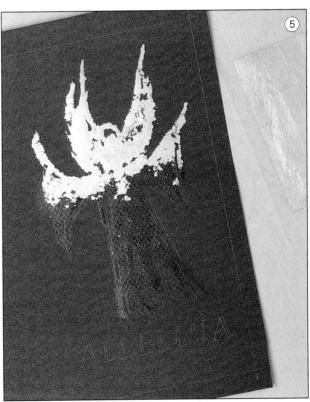

7 Make a matching envelope, adapting the basic template on page 47.

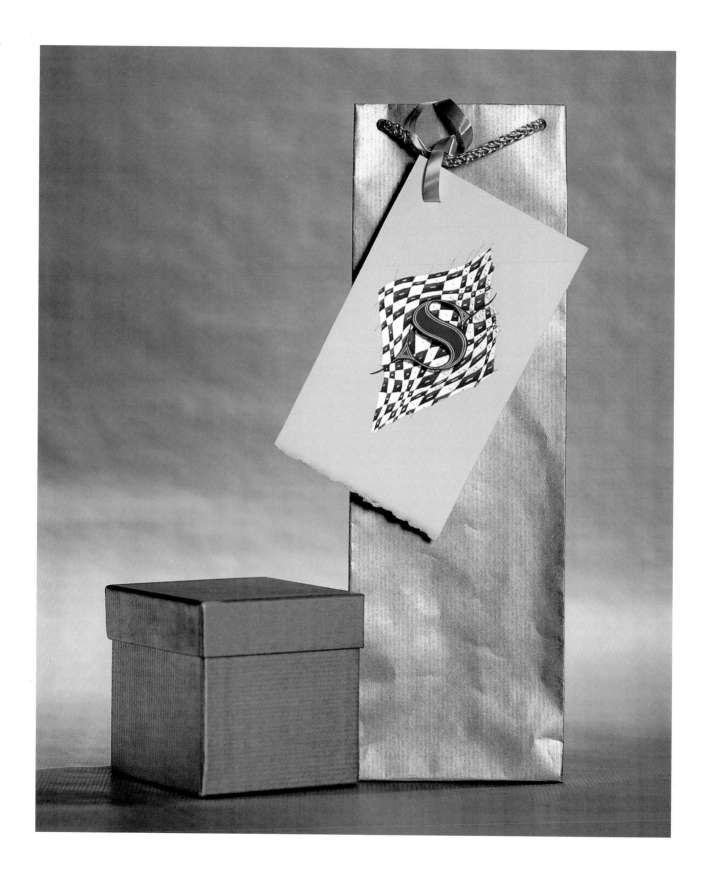

gilded and decorated letter

Here is a traditional idea taken from old manuscripts and given a modern flavour, using gold leaf on gum ammoniac to make an attractive framed piece, or used as a gift tag. I have chosen a Lombardic style versal letter (see page 31) for my model here. These letters have voluptuous curves, which lend themselves to decoration, and the serifs can also be extended to add to the decorative possibilities. Choose the appropriate letter for the name of the recipient of the gift.

specific materials

Essential equipment (see pages 8–9)
Dip pen and fine pointed drawing nib
Gouache, French ultramarine, scarlet lake,
    cadmium yellow, opaque white and black
Coloured pencils, in similar shades to gouache
1 sheet HP watercolour paper, 300 gsm
Waterproof black ink, well diluted
Gum ammoniac solution
Synthetic brush, No. 0
Scalpel, cutting mat and metal ruler
Brushes and palette for mixing gouache
Sable brushes, Nos 3, 0, 00 and 000
Ballpoint pen

finished size of letter and background

70 x 65 mm ($2\frac{3}{4}$ x $2\frac{1}{2}$ in)

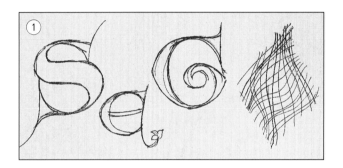

1 Draft out your chosen letter shape on layout paper at actual size, then consider the scale of the background diamond pattern and draw this out too (1). I have chosen to twist the pattern as though it were folded fabric, which produces some interesting shapes.

2 Use coloured pencils to fill in the pattern to see how the shapes work. Trace the letter shape and lay this over the coloured pattern, moving the trace around until you find an area that looks good behind the letter (2). You may have to make some adjustments to the twisted pattern to get it just right. Use card strips to decide the margins around the letter and mark them on your tracing.

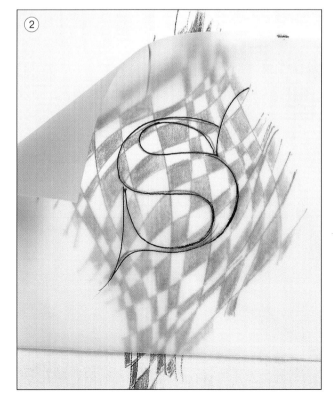

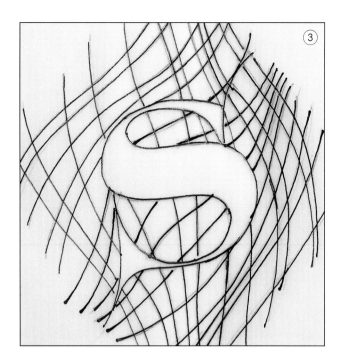

(3)

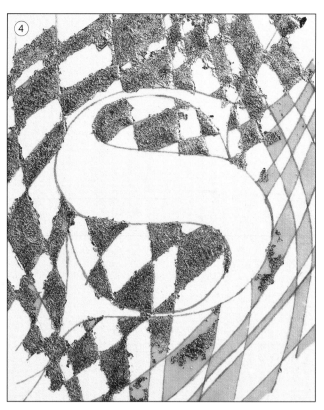

(4)

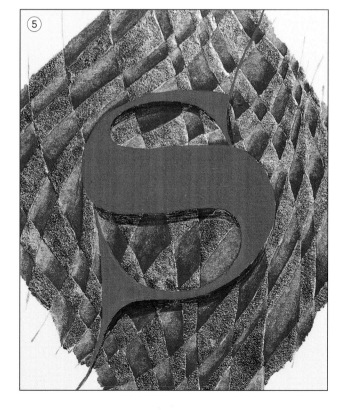

(5)

3 When you are satisfied that the design hangs together well, go over letter and background pattern onto a fresh sheet of tracing paper (3), then transfer it to watercolour paper (see page 36), allowing plenty of space all round for margins.

4 Go over the traced lines with very well diluted waterproof ink and a pointed nib, erasing any visible pencil lines carefully when the ink is dry. When you paint over the lines, ink will not repel or mix with the paint as pencil carbon would.

5 Do the gilding first. Stir the gum ammoniac solution thoroughly, then, following your colour sketch and using a No. 0 synthetic brush, lay an even layer over the appropriate areas. Try to avoid getting bubbles when laying the gum and allow it to dry for about 30 minutes. Apply two layers of gold leaf as described on page 64, making sure that all the gum is completely covered (4). Burnish gently between applications through glassine.

6 Clean off surplus gold with a soft brush and tidy up any rough edges with a pointed scalpel blade before polishing with a piece of soft silk. Mix up some French ultramarine and paint in the remaining diamonds, using a No. 0 or 00 sable brush as appropriate (5).

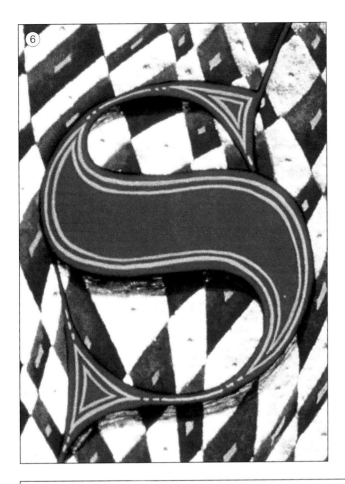

7 Draw in the outline of the letter using a No. 00 sable brush and a mixture of scarlet lake plus a little cadmium yellow. Use this fine brush to fill in the narrow parts of the letter, but switch to a No. 3 for the rest, painting in generous sweeps (5). Keep the colour moving and add more paint to the brush as necessary. If you paint wet into wet, you should get a nice even layer of colour.

8 Mix black gouache with a little French ultramarine and paint an outline around the letter with a No. 000 brush. A very steady hand is required, although any tiny wobbles can be painted over, if necessary. With the same brush and colour, paint in fine, hairline strokes to form a "shadow" beneath the letter, then blend these strokes together with a dampened No. 3 brush.

9 Add highlights with opaque white, a No. 000 sable brush and the steady hand already mentioned. Indent dots in the centre of each gold diamond with a ballpoint pen through a piece of glassine, to add an extra twinkle (6). Use a craft knife or hole punch to make a slit/hole for the ribbon in the top corner. If you want to frame the finished piece, cut a bevel-edged mount according to the margins you chose in step 2, which keeps the gold from coming into contact with the glass of the frame.

For the project, the letter was kept fairly plain as it sits on a busy background of blue and gold diamonds. An alternative could be a rather more elaborately decorated letter on a plain gilded background, created in the same way: gilding first, then paint the letter, and finally add the outline and white decorations.

For the dotted lines over the gold, work out the pattern on the original tracing first. Cover the work with glassine, lay tracing over this and tack down with masking tape. Follow the tracing and transfer the dotted lines using a ballpoint against a ruler to keep the lines straight, pressing quite hard to make a reasonable impression through the two layers onto the gold. Draw in small diamonds freehand within the dotted shapes.

The flourished "tails" are drawn in last of all, with gouache in a fine pointed nib. Practise the flourishes on paper first, then draw them straight onto the work freehand. Tracing them down first is unsatisfactory as the results often look stiff. Just have courage and go for it!

variation

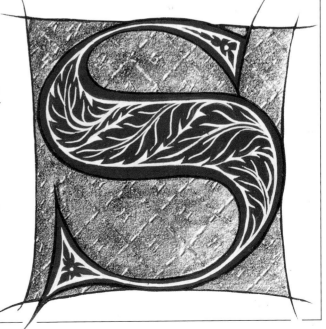

alphabet and
gilded a-z

This project develops your early experiments with combining alphabets and flourished italics and adds a gold focal point, which is written with a card "pen". When framed it will make an attractive piece.

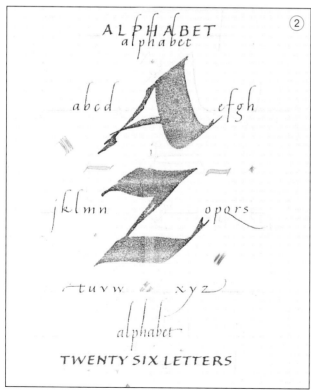

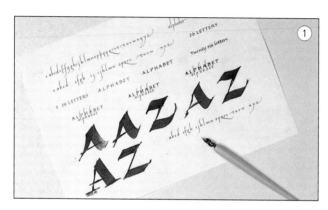

specific materials

Essential equipment (see pages 8–9)
Dip pen and nibs, Nos $3\frac{1}{2}$ and 5
Repositionable glue
Gum ammoniac solution
Coloured pencils, black, red and gold
1 sheet Ingres paper, 160 gsm, black
Gouache, scarlet lake
Schmincke Tro-col bronze (pale gold, powdered gouache)
Brushes and palette for mixing gouache
Scrap card, to use as a "pen"
Gilding equipment (see page 64)
White pencil (optional)
Scalpel, cutting mat and metal ruler
Acid-free card, 1 mm ($\frac{1}{32}$ in) thick
Bone folder

finished size overall
260 x 190 mm ($10\frac{1}{4}$ x $7\frac{1}{2}$ in)

size of cut out
175 x 110 mm ($8\frac{7}{8}$ x $4\frac{3}{8}$ in)

1 Do some thumbnail sketches and then write out the various elements of the piece in black ink on layout paper, experimenting with nib and letter sizes and weights (1).

2 Make one or more paste-up layouts of promising designs (use photocopies so you won't need to write things out more than once), deciding the margins with the help of card strips. Redraw your chosen layout (2).

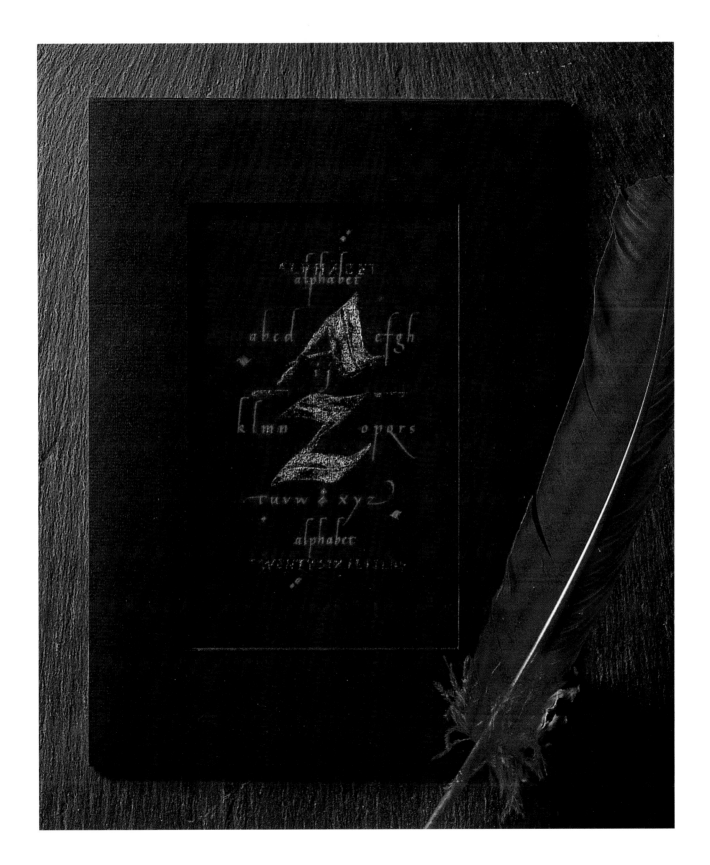

3 Photocopy your layout (or work on the original if you prefer) and use coloured pencils to get an idea of the colour balance and where you could perhaps add a flourish or two to complete the design (3).

4 Do some trials on a small piece of black Ingres paper (using the laid surface) (4). Use a pen to write the words in gum ammoniac. To give a little twinkle to the scarlet gouache, drop in a very small amount of Tro-col powder as you mix it, stirring each time you load your nib. The laid texture which gives an interesting effect with the large gold letters will cause some problems when writing with a fine nib. You can flatten the laid lines with a bone folder, although this makes the paper shiny. Either accept a few imprecise lines and tidy them up, using a scalpel for the gilding or a fine brush for the red letters, or use the smooth side of the paper.

5 Use a card "pen" (see page 60) to practise writing in the large A and Z with gum ammoniac. Before the gum solution dries out, scrape a line (straight, wavy or zigzag) into it with a paintbrush handle and leave to dry completely. Gild the words and the A and Z as usual (see page 64).

6 Draw out the rectangle (with trim allowance) on the black paper and rule it up lightly. Follow the line lengths on the paste-up accurately to minimize the amount of erasing necessary. You may wish to use the carbon method (see page 36) with a white pencil to transfer the letters to be gilded.

7 Gild the letters as practised in Step 4. Mix up some fresh red gouache and Tro-col powder and write in the remaining parts of the design (5). You will have found from your experiments that the gold powder gives an interesting speckled finish. To make the most of this effect, write only about two letters at a time, rinse the nib, remix the paint, reapply to the nib and carry on in this way until you have finished. It may seem a little laborious, but without this extra effort, the letters will end up plain red.

8 Trim out the piece with a scalpel and metal ruler, then draw out and cut a rectangle of the same size from acid-free card. Attach the finished piece to the card rectangle with a dab of glue at each corner.

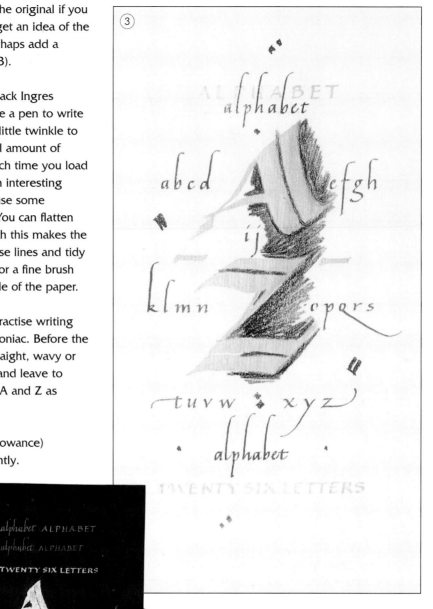

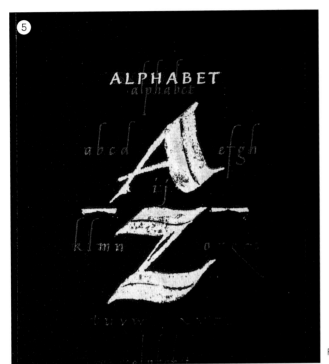

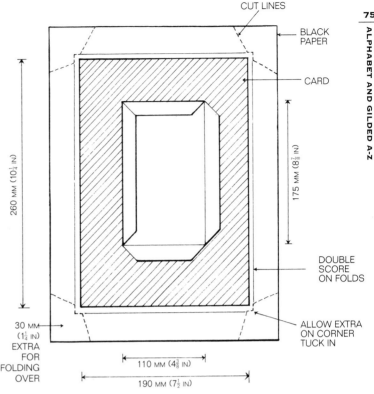

CUT LINES

BLACK PAPER

CARD

260 MM (10¼ IN)

175 MM (8⅞ IN)

DOUBLE SCORE ON FOLDS

30 MM (1¼ IN) EXTRA FOR FOLDING OVER

ALLOW EXTRA ON CORNER TUCK IN

110 MM (4⅜ IN)

190 MM (7½ IN)

to make a paper-covered mount

1 Use another sheet of card and Ingres paper to make a mount. Cut out a rectangle of card as large as your frame. Draw up and cut out a window in the card, to correspond with the position of the image. Top and side margins should be the same, the bottom one slightly deeper.

2 Cut a rectangle of Ingres paper, about 30 mm (1¼ in) larger all round than the card, making sure the laid lines go in the same direction as on the finished piece. You will also need to cut a narrow strip, 1 mm (1/32 in) wide, pieces of which should be stuck into the corners of the window to eliminate any white showing when the flaps are folded round.

3 Draw out a rectangle the size of the item being framed (here, 260 x 190 mm/10¼ x 7½ in) on the reverse side of the black paper and another rectangle 1 mm (1/32 in) larger all round, then score them both – this allows the paper to be folded easily over the thickness of the card (6). Repeat the process for the hole in the middle.

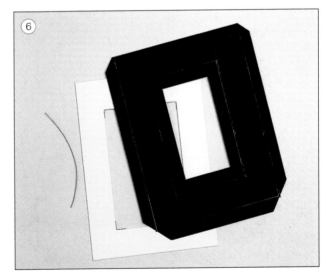

4 Put dabs of glue in the card mount corners and stick it down onto the back of the black paper, matching corner marks.

5 Follow the diagram (above) for cutting inner mitres and outer corners. With clean scrap paper underneath, glue each flap and smooth down onto the mount, tucking in the outer corners with a bone folder.

a magic carpet:
gilding with colour

This simple technique, using coloured size under gold leaf, which is etched back to reveal the colours, yields interesting results which make attractive presents. I have based my design on Oriental carpets, but there are many other possibilities.

specific materials

Essential equipment (see pages 8–9)

1 sheet HP watercolour paper, 300 gsm

Gouache, dark but bright colours that show
   up well against gold, for example scarlet lake,
   French ultramarine and viridian

PVA glue

Distilled water

Gum ammoniac solution

Synthetic brushes and palette for mixing coloured gesso

Gilding equipment (see page 64)

6H pencil

Scalpel

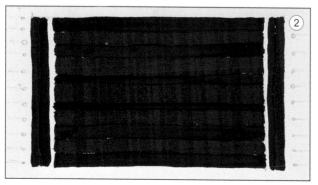

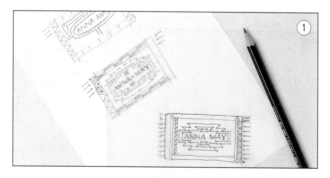

finished size

30 x 74 mm ($1\frac{1}{8}$ x $1\frac{3}{4}$ in)

1 Devise a pattern to scratch into a gilded surface to reveal the colour beneath, sketching your ideas out on tracing paper at full size. Designs can be quickly modified by laying over another sheet and tracing off; you also have the design ready to transfer onto the gilding (1).

2 Transfer the outline of your design to watercolour paper (see page 36).

3 Make a coloured gesso by squeezing out about 6 mm ($\frac{1}{4}$ in) of gouache and combining it with 4 drops of PVA mixed 50/50 with distilled water, 4 drops of gum ammoniac mixed 50/50 with distilled water, and 4 drops of undiluted PVA glue. Use the end of a paintbrush to measure out the drops, and aim to keep them all roughly the same size. Mix to a smooth, stiff consistency, repeating the formula for each colour you want to use in separate palette wells. It is possible to keep this gesso from drying out too quickly by covering the palette tightly with plastic food wrap (cling film).

4 Use a synthetic brush to apply the coloured gesso. First experiment on scrap paper with alternating stripes, squares of different sizes and other motifs. Then paint your chosen design on watercolour paper. There's no need to be too precise, so draw the shapes in freehand. Aim to apply an even, flat layer: this is quite difficult as the mixture is rather sticky, but try to avoid getting too many lumps and bubbles. Cover the full design area with colour and add the "tassels" with gum ammoniac and then leave to dry completely (2).

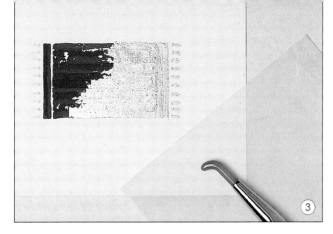

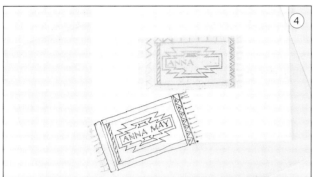

5 Cover the entire coloured area with at least two layers of transfer gold leaf (see page 64) (3). Burnish well through glassine.

6 Lay your tracing over the gold surface and go over the design lines using firm pressure with a 6H pencil. Don't be too precise, just transfer the bones of your layout and let the design evolve as you work through step 7.

7 Remove the tracing paper and scratch the pattern into the gold with a scalpel to reveal the colour, but not so hard that you go through to the paper (4).

8 When you have completed the scratched design, clean off the surplus colour and gold with a soft brush and then polish the gold gently with a piece of soft silk. If framing behind glass the piece should be mounted to keep the gold away from the glass.

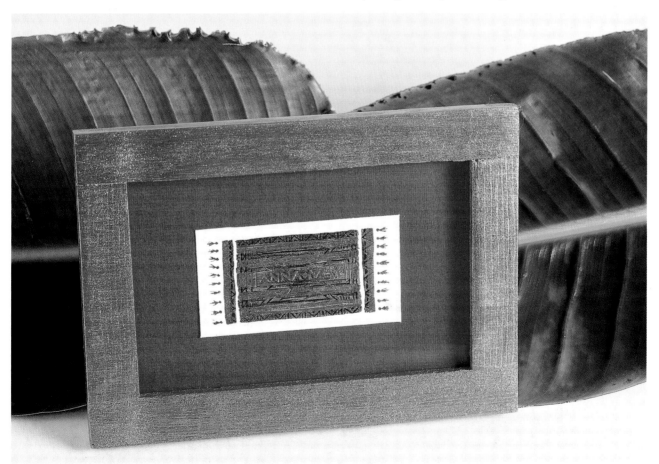

glossary

ARMENIAN BOLE Red-brown earth pigment.

ASCENDER Part of the lower case letter extending above the x-height.

BASELINE Line on which letters are written.

BLEED Occurs when the paper surface absorbs ink or paint.

BODY HEIGHT Main part of the letter, also known as the x-height.

BONE FOLDER Flat piece of bone, round at one end, pointed at the other. Used for scoring and folding paper.

BROAD-EDGED NIB Produces thick and thin strokes by writing at a constant angle, not by pressure.

BURNISH To polish gold leaf to a glossy finish, usually through glassine to protect the leaf.

BURNISHER Tool used to burnish gold leaf. Can be made of agate, haematite or psilomelanite.

CAPITAL Majuscule or uppercase letter.

COMPLEMENTARY COLOUR Each primary colour has a complementary colour made by mixing the other two primaries.

DESCENDER Part of the lower case letter extending below the baseline.

EXEMPLAR A model alphabet or piece of work for students to study.

FORM Abbreviation of letterform, meaning the actual shape of the letter.

GESSO A mixture or solution laid as a base for gilding.

GLASSINE Transparent, non-stick paper used to protect work in progress, as an overlay for finished work and in gilding.

GOUACHE Opaque water-based paint, also known as body colour.

GRAIN In paper, direction in which most of the fibres lie.

GUM AMMONIAC Plant resin. Can be soaked in water to make size for gilding. Also available as a ready-mixed solution.

GUM ARABIC Plant resin. A drop or two of the solution added to paint helps it flow and gives a slight sheen to the paint when dry. If there is little gum in the tube of paint, it will not adhere properly to the paper.

GUM SANDARACH Plant resin. Ground fine and applied to paper, it is a water repellent. Useful on absorbent paper to prevent bleed.

HAND Another way of describing a letter style, for example, the italic hand.

INTERLINEAR SPACE Space between two lines of writing, usually measured by the x-height.

LAYOUT Arrangement of heading, text, illustration and any other elements in a piece of work.

LETTERFORM Actual shape of the letter.

LIGATURE Linking strokes between letters.

LOWER CASE Typographical term for small letters or minuscules.

MAJUSCULES Capital or uppercase letter.

MINUSCULES Small or lower case letters that have ascenders and descenders.

MONOLINE Letters made with strokes of a single nib-width or drawn with single pencil lines, also called skeleton letters. The essence of the letterform.

OX GALL In liquid form, add sparingly to mixed paint to improve flow from pen or brush.

PASTE-UP Assembled cut-up elements of a piece of work are stuck onto paper to finalize the layout.

PEN ANGLE Angle at which the pen meets the paper in relation to the writing line.

POUNCE Powdered pumice, used to remove grease from paper.

PVA Polyvinylacetate, a glue.

SERIF Stroke that leads into or finishes a letter.

SHADE OF A COLOUR Made by adding black in graded amounts to any given colour.

SIZE Glue added to paper pulp or applied to the surface of a finished sheet to make it less absorbent to ink or paint. Also a sticky base to which gold leaf will adhere.

SKELETON LETTER Letter made without the calligraphic weight of a broad-edged nib. Also known as monoline.

STEM Main vertical stroke of a letter.

STROKE Component of a letter made without lifting the pen from the writing surface.

TONE OR TONAL VALUE Gradation from light to dark, visible in any solid object viewed in the light. Best seen by half-closing the eyes.

TOOTH Very slight surface texture of paper, which prevents the nib from slipping.

UPPERCASE Typographic term for capital letters or majuscules.

WEIGHT Relationship of the nib-width to the height of a letter.

WET-AND-DRY PAPER Abrasive paper available in several grades. The finer grades are useful for nib sharpening. Available from DIY stores or motor accessory shops.

X-HEIGHT Main part or body height of the letter, not including the ascender or descender.

useful addresses

Atlantis
7–9 Plummers Row
London E1 1EQ
Tel: 020 7377 8855
Papers for calligraphy and painting.
Paints and brushes. Mail order service.

L Cornelissen & Son Ltd
105 Great Russell Street
London WC1B 3RY.
Tel: 020 7636 105
E-mail for orders:
orders@cornelissen.com
E-mail for information:
enquiries@cornelissen.com
Pens, nibs, pencils, brushes, paints and
inks. Gum arabic and gum ammoniac in
crystalline form. Also gilding supplies.

Cowling & Wilcox
26–28 Broadwick Street
London
W1F 8HX
Tel: 020 7734 5781
Fax: 020 7434 4513
www.cowlingandwilcox.com
General art supplies.

Daler Rowney
Southern Industrial Area
PO Box 10
Bracknell, Berkshire RG12 8ST
Tel: 01344 424621
Manufacturers of pens, nibs, pencils,
brushes, paints and inks. Contact for
nearest stockist.

Duchy Gilding Company
The Old Mortuary Studio
13 Gyllyng Street
Falmouth, Cornwall TR11 3EL
Tel: 01326 211692
Gilding supplies. Mail order only.

Falkiner Fine Papers
76 Southampton Row
London WC1B 4AR
Tel: 020 7831 1151

Specialist papers for calligraphy,
watercolour and bookbinding. Pens,
nibs, liquid and stick ink, ink stones,
bone folders, book-binding
equipment, gum sandarach crystals,
pounce, burnishers. Mail order service.

W Habberley Meadows Ltd
5 Saxon Way
Chelmsley Wood
Birmingham B35 5AY
Tel: 0121 770 0103
www.habberleymeadows.co.uk
Gilding supplies.

R Jackson & Sons Ltd
20 Slater Street
Liverpool L1 4BS
Tel: 0151 709 2647
Wide variety of materials for
calligraphy and painting.

T N Lawrence
117–119 Clerkenwell Road
London EC1R 5BY (shop only)
Tel: 020 7242 3534
www.lawrence.co.uk
Huge range of papers as well as other
artist's materials. Website features the
full range of products with shopping
basket facility.

Penmandirect
Martin Taylor
1 Towneley Road West
Longridge, Lancashire PR3 3AB.
Tel/fax: 01772 78444
Wide variety of calligraphic materials.
UK mail order only.

Winsor & Newton
Whitefriars Avenue
Harrow, Middlesex HA3 5RH
Tel: 020 8427 4343.
www.winsornewton.com
Manufacturers of pens, nibs, pencils,
brushes, paints and inks. Contact for
nearest stockist .

Wrights of Lymm Ltd
Wright House
Millers Lane
Lymm, Cheshire WA13 9RG
Tel: 01925 752226
Gilding supplies.

calligraphic societies

National societies with an international
membership. Regular journals and
newsletters keep members up to
date. Both societies have affiliated
regional groups. Contact numbers
and addresses are given for further
information about study courses
and other events.

Society of Scribes and Illuminators
(The first calligraphic society,
founded in 1921)
6 Queen Square
London WC1N 3AR
E-mail: scribe@calligraphy.org
www.calligraphy.org

Calligraphy and Lettering Arts Society
54 Boileau Road
London SW13 9BL
E-mail:
suecavendish@compuserve.com

bibliography

Writing & Illuminating & Lettering
Edward Johnston, A & C Black, 1906

Pen Lettering
Ann Camp, A & C Black, 1984

A Book of Scripts
Alfred Fairbank, Faber & Faber, 1977

The Calligrapher's Handbook
Ed. Heather Child, A & C Black, 1985

index